reading aids series

READING FOR PLEASURE:

guidelines

Dixie Lee Spiegel
University of North Carolina at Chapel Hill

1981

Clearing House on Reading and Communication Skills
National Institute of Education

International Reading Association
800 Barksdale Road, Newark, Delaware 19711

Library of Congress Cataloging in Publication Data
Spiegel, Dixie Lee, 1942-
   Reading for pleasure.

   (Reading aids series)
   Includes bibliographical references.
   1. Books and reading for children—United States.
I. Title. II. Series.
Z1037.S7576   028.5   81-8395
ISBN O-87207-226-6   AACR2

CONTENTS

Foreword   *v*

Preface   *vii*

THEORY

2   Importance of a Recreational Reading Program
     As an Adjunct to a Regular Reading Program   *4*
     As a Way of Enhancing Important Aspects of Reading Development   *7*
        Development of Positive Attitudes toward Reading   *7*
        Expansion of Experiental Background   *11*
        Practice in Decoding Strategies: Development of Automaticity   *12*
        Development of the Use of Context Clues   *14*
        Development of a Meaning Vocabulary   *15*
     In Conclusion   *17*

18   Research on Recreational Reading
      References   *22*

PRACTICE

26   Motivating Students to Read for Pleasure
      Teacher Attitudes   *27*
      Grouping Procedures   *31*
      Expanding Reading Interests   *36*
        The Appropriateness of Using a Recreational Reading Program to
           Expand Interests   *36*
        Encouraging Children to Widen Their Reading Interests   *37*
        Sharing Reading with Others   *45*

51 Initiating a Recreational Reading Program
 Preparing the Environment *51*
 Preparing the Students *53*
 Preparing Parents *57*
  Making the Initial Contact *57*
  Suggestions for Support at Home *58*
  Suggestions for Support at School *61*
 Preparing the Administration *62*

64 Managing Time for Recreational Reading
 Slipping Recreational Reading into the Schedule *64*
 Revising Existing Practices and Schedules *66*
 Transferring Recreational Reading to the Home Front *68*

70 Managing Materials for a Recreational Reading Program
 Maintaining a Classroom Library *70*
  Sources of Materials *71*
  Selecting Materials *72*
  Keeping a Classroom Library Circulating *76*
 Enlisting the Cooperation of the School Librarian *79*
  Library Procedures to Enhance Recreational Reading *80*
  Motivational Activities for Librarians *81*
 Finding Materials for Children's Personal Libraries *83*
  RIF *83*
  Other Ways to Augment Home Libraries *84*

86 Keeping Track of It All
 References *87*

FOREWORD

What does it profit children to learn a skill which they have little or no motivation to use? It seems to be true that learning the skill must come first, for without it most children and adults will not often read voluntarily simply because the act of doing so involves too much work.

But why do so many persons who have attained considerable skill choose not to take advantage of the wealth of information and pleasure which resides in print? Is it at least partly because we have not provided enough time or presented enough inducements in school to help children form the lifelong habit which is so important? Perhaps we have not worked hard enough with libraries and with parents to coordinate efforts designed to help children realize what they will miss if they do not voluntarily read.

This volume, cooperatively developed with ERIC/RCS, provides many helpful suggestions. It is for the classroom teachers and the administrators who want their schools to reflect commitment to the idea that reading for pleasure is an essential part of every successful reading program.

Olive S. Niles, *President*
International Reading Association
1980-1981

vi

PREFACE

The Educational Resources Information Center (ERIC) is a national information system developed by the U.S. Office of Education and now sponsored by the National Institute of Education (NIE). It provides ready access to descriptions of exemplary programs, research and development efforts, and related information useful in developing more effective educational programs.

Through its network of specialized centers or clearinghouses, each of which is responsible for a particular educational area, ERIC acquires, evaluates, abstracts, and indexes current significant information and lists this information in its reference publications.

ERIC/RCS, the ERIC Clearinghouse on Reading and Communication Skills, disseminates educational information related to research, instruction, and personnel preparation at all levels and in all institutions. The scope of interest of the Clearinghouse includes relevant research reports, literature reviews, curriculum guides and descriptions, conference papers, project or program reviews, and other print materials related to all aspects of reading, English, educational journalism, and speech communication.

The ERIC system has already made available—through the ERIC Document Reproduction System—much informative data. However, if the findings of specific educational research are to be intelligible to teachers and applicable to teaching, considerable bodies of data must be reevaluated, focused, translated, and molded into an essentially different context. Rather than resting at the point of making research reports readily accessible, NIE has directed the separate clearinghouses to work with professional organizations in developing information analysis papers in specific areas within the scope of the clearinghouses.

ERIC is pleased to cooperate with the International Reading Association in making *Reading for Pleasure: Guidelines* available.

Bernard O'Donnell
Director, ERIC/RCS

THEORY

IMPORTANCE OF A
RECREATIONAL READING PROGRAM

As a former special reading teacher who dealt primarily with children having trouble with reading, one of my biggest concerns was that few of these children would ever really *like* reading. Reading for many of these children would be associated with failure, humiliation, and just plain hard work. The thought of voluntarily picking up an instrument of such torture would rarely occur to them.

Unfortunately, much evidence has been found to show that such a gloomy prognosis may be warranted. In a 1978 survey done by the Book Industry Study Group, 6 percent of those interviewed reported never reading anything at all (LeGrand-Brodsky, 1979). Nothing. Not even the newspaper. Of the 94 percent who were reading, 39 percent never read a book. Their reading was limited mainly to magazines and newspapers. And of the remaining 55 percent of "book readers," only 33 percent reported reading as much as one book a month (Yankelovich, 1978).

Another study (Greaney and Quinn, 1978) found 22 percent of those responding never read and of those who did read, 23 percent read less than 55 minutes a day. In contrast to the Book Industry survey, this study found only 7 percent of reading time was spent with newspapers and 62 percent was spent in reading books.

A third study is no more encouraging. Surveys by the National Opinion Research Center led to the estimate that approximately 10 percent of the United States population reads 80 percent of the books read. Furthermore, this group found that half of the adult population in the sample admitted to having never read a book all the way through (Gallup, 1972).

As reading educators we should all be concerned about why people don't read. Of course some don't because they can't, at least not with ease. Others profess not to have enough time. (And yet those of us who are compulsive readers know you can always snatch the time—while doing the dishes, drying your hair, ironing. I even tried reading while mowing the lawn, but the vibrations defeated me.) In the Book Industry study, 28 percent of the nonreaders said they didn't read because they just didn't like it (LeGrand-Brodsky, 1979). Sadly, that 28 percent who admitted they didn't even want to read probably represent a conservative estimate. They were the ones who were forthright enough to admit it.

How is it that thousands of teachers in the United States have been unable to instill in their students a love of reading, a love that probably the majority of these teachers have themselves? LeGrand-Brodsky suggests one answer: "Generally speaking [these nonreaders] have never gained the reading experience necessary to develop an interest in, or ability to enjoy, reading books or other materials" (p. 948). In this monograph I hope to present ideas that will help classroom teachers provide the experiences children need in order to develop both the skill in reading and the love of reading that will cause them to choose it as an enjoyable leisure-time activity.

This monograph deals with recreational reading—why it is important and how teachers can manage a recreational reading program in their schools and classrooms. Recreational reading will be defined as voluntary reading of self-selected materials, either for information or for pleasure. The final goal of a recreational reading program is that students will enjoy reading and seek it as an activity. The process of reaching this final goal may necessarily begin with nonvoluntary reading but, unless the students make the transfer from reading during teacher-ordained time to reading voluntarily, the program is not really a success.

A recreational reading program should not be confused with an individualized reading program. An individualized reading program does involve a great deal of self-selected, self-paced reading. However, whereas a recreational reading program is concerned primarily with the *practice* of learned skills, an individualized reading program also deals with the development and monitoring of these skills or abilities. A well-conceived individualized program should be a total developmental reading program; a recreational reading program makes no such claims. It is an adjunct to a reading program.

The development of a love of reading is too important to be left to chance. A recreational reading program should be a conscious, planned part of every classroom program. This is true for two major reasons. First, the nature of many developmental reading programs militates against voluntary reading for enjoyment. Second, recreational reading helps the development of several crucial aspects of successful reading. It promotes positive attitudes toward reading, expands experiential background, enhances automaticity and fluency, provides opportunity for practice in the use of context clues, and expands meaning vocabularies.

As an Adjunct to a Regular Reading Program

Many developmental reading programs are very structured. The most common method of organizing such a program is to use a basal reading program. Basal reading programs have become very complete and complex, and the teacher must coordinate the suggestions in the teacher's manual with workbook activities, ditto pages, skills assessment, and related multimedia offerings. Some teachers (misguidedly) feel they must have their students do *all* of the activities for each story. Even teachers who are selective find that children may be completely overwhelmed with finishing one-page skill activities. As a result, the students may rarely have a chance to read. That is, they read their assigned stories and sometimes their ditto sheets, but they don't have much time to sit back, relax, and put to use all this wonderful knowledge about reading. Allington (1977) reports informal observations that poor readers, especially, have very little opportunity to actually *read* during instruction. His observations found that poor readers read a mean of 43 words in context per lesson. This finding caused him to ask: "If, in a typical week of reading instruction, students only encounter 150 to 500 words in context, one has to ask how they will ever get good" (p. 58). An additional danger is that children will spend so much time doing assigned reading that they will perceive reading simply as an assignment. Furthermore, they don't get sufficient time just to practice their reading. Teachers using basal programs should seriously consider giving up some of the "purple plague" activities they assign their students and replacing them with a more meaningful kind of practice—free reading.

Many basal programs are now including a skills management system as one of their components. Whether teachers use basal-related or independent skills management systems they must be wary of becoming too involved in measuring and developing reading skills that can be described objectively. Affective factors, such as reading for enjoyment, are often difficult to describe in objective terms and may be overlooked in the rush to check off tidily-arranged skills lists. Teachers using skills-management systems need to be aware of this hazard. Perhaps they might view recreational reading as a logical and necessary fourth step: pretest-teach-posttest-provide opportunities for application during free reading. This fourth step would not only provide built-in opportunities for the students to practice what the teacher has preached; it would also build in a much needed gasp-for-breath in the headlong pace of mastering reading skills. I suspect that many developers of skills management systems would applaud this fourth step as a way to combat the abuses which often surround skills management systems.

Teachers who use the Language Experience Approach (LEA) may be more inclined to include recreational reading as an integral part of their reading program than teachers who use more structured programs. Because numerous skills activities are not prescribed by a manual and because the reading material consists only of what the children themselves write, most teachers just naturally have the children practice their reading on additional published materials—old basal readers, trade books, or even newspapers. Often the children themselves initiate this additional reading. They want to show that they can read from "real" books. As a result, LEA teachers do not find it difficult to incorporate recreational reading into the daily routine. They simply have to be sure that a wide variety of suitable materials is readily available and that children have opportunities to use them.

The one kind of reading program that almost guarantees a high degree of free reading is the individualized program. The students select their own reading materials and progress through them at their own pace. Skill development is usually done through teacher-pupil conferences or through ad hoc skill groups. In spite of this emphasis on free choice in reading, even the individualized approach has some potential pitfalls. First, the reading is not really "free," in the sense that the student is usually accountable in some way for everything read. (More about this later.) Second, the free reading may be perceived by the student as "what I do during reading class." That is, as with a basal text, the reading is an assigned task, even though the choice of what to read is left to the student.

The point of all this discussion about various reading programs is not to advocate one kind of program over another. Rather, the point is that regardless of the kind of reading program used, teachers need to make conscious plans for having recreational reading as a very real part of the reading program. Unless a commitment is made to recreational reading, it will be all too easy to let that aspect of reading slip away, to let it be the first part of the program to be replaced when "more important" work needs to be done.

As a Way of Enhancing Important Aspects
of Reading Development

The development of students who both can and will read should be the ultimate goal of any reading program. Serendipitously, recreational reading not only allows the students to behave as though they had already reached this ultimate goal, but also aids the process of reaching the goal.

Development of Positive Attitudes toward Reading

McCracken and McCracken (1978) have contributed much to the concept of Sustained Silent Reading (SSR), first introduced by Hunt (1970) as USSR (in which U = Uninterrupted). During SSR students read materials of their own choice for a specified amount of time. No interruptions are allowed and the teacher is also to be doing leisure reading at this time. McCracken and McCracken (p. 408) have identified seven positive messages about reading that children can learn from participating in SSR. These positive messages can be found in any good recreational reading program that allows self-selection and reading in more than short snatches of time.

1. *Reading books is important.* As Oliver points out (1973), children develop a sense of what the teacher values by noting what the teacher chooses to have them do. Children who daily must fight their way through a purple blizzard of ditto sheets will very likely perceive reading as filling in vowel letters and underlining main ideas. Children who read only basal reader length stories will perceive reading as related only to stories 5-10 pages long. If teachers want their students to develop into individuals who choose to read fully developed pieces of literature, whether narrative or expository, they must allow children to read those kinds of materials. Furthermore, this kind of reading must be a valued part of the curriculum, not just a "when-you-are-done-with-everything-else" part. Let's face it—poor readers would never get to read anything longer than a basal story if free reading were relegated to the limbo of a reward for completing all other assignments.

2. *Reading is something anyone can do.* Athey (1978) warns that teachers must start very early helping children to realize that reading is something they can do and something that should have value in their lives: "We must be sure that the self as reader is not one of those that is discarded during these important years" (p. 2).

Hunt (1970) points out that if SSR is combined with teacher-pupil conferences the teacher may, through adroit questioning, help students develop concepts of themselves as readers and perceptions of what a good reader is. Questions such as "Did you read better today than yesterday?" "Did you have the feeling of wanting to go ahead faster to find out what happened?" and "Were you always counting to see how many pages you had to go?" should help to make readers aware of how they are developing as readers (pp. 148-149).

The noncompetitive aspect of recreational reading is important for developing the concept that everyone can read. Even in a supposedly homogeneous basal reading group, some readers are always better than others. And intragroup comparisons are always made, in spite of teacher attempts to minimize the differences. One great advantage of including a component of recreational reading in any reading program is described by McCracken (1971, p. 582): "Poor readers respond that since no one watches them they can make mistakes without worrying. Able readers say that they are relieved that they don't have to prove that they are bright every time they read something." When one is allowed to choose one's own material and read at one's own rate, reading truly is something anyone can do.

3. *Reading is communicating with an author.* Reading short snatches of material, and then only when so directed, can interfere with the understanding that reading means communicating with the author. Rather, reading may be perceived as communicating with the teacher. One of the most exciting offshoots of a recreational reading program can be the freedom to react as an individual to the message of an author without worrying whether you have the "right" reaction. (Remember those ghastly literature classes in which teachers tried to get the class to appreciate the same esoteric messages they received? *You* liked

the story for something quite different and it was deflating to find out your quite natural, spontaneous reaction was "wrong.")

4. *Children are capable of sustained thought.* One of the concerns of many teachers is that children don't seem to be able to stick with anything for very long. A lot of children are characterized by what I call "butterfly brains"—they flit merrily from topic to topic. And yet the ways in which many school days are organized encourages such flightiness. A classroom teacher must teach reading, spelling, composition, grammar, social studies, math, and science. All this is sandwiched between music, band practice, visits to the speech pathologist, special units on Fire Prevention, and assemblies. Furthermore, many of the published materials are divided into small segments. Primary grade teachers are especially familiar with the disheartening phenomenon of taking more time to explain an activity than it takes for the children to do it. No wonder children don't seem capable of sustained thought. They have pitifully few opportunities to practice it.

Children seem to welcome the periods of sustained activity that come with SSR. Several reports of SSR programs (e.g., McCracken, 1971; Petre, 1971) have mentioned the students' positive reaction to this quiet time of the day. Not only do the students have no trouble sustaining reading for long periods, they actually look forward to the peacefulness—the "down time"— that surrounds this part of the day. Surely most teachers enjoy this tranquility too.

5. *Books are meant to be read in large sections.* One of the silliest practices to be observed in many basal classrooms is that of restricting children to reading only the assigned portions of the story. After expending a great deal of energy to motivate the children to *want* to read the story, some teachers will even chastise students for "reading ahead." Stories are not meant to be read in 3-page segments!

Ley (1979) points out that even SSR periods can work against the idea that book reading involves large chunks of time. One common practice is to have an entire school "shut down" for SSR for 30 minutes once a week. However, Ley cautions that providing for sustained reading only once a week is not enough "because it does not provide consecutive days for reading the same book, and students often lose interest (or lose the book) before they have finished it" (p. 24).

6. *Teachers believe that the pupils are comprehending (because they don't bother to check).* One of the recurrent themes of this manuscript will be: If children only read because you require them to and if you don't believe that they have read unless they produce a product, then you have not had a successful recreational reading program. I am continually horrified when teachers ask me, "But how do you know they've read it if they don't have to make a report about it?" Coercion does not induce volunteers. No child ever learned to love reading by writing book reports. Or drawing pictures of exciting events. Or creating a six-act play about the story. Some children may enjoy some of these activities, but I seriously doubt that knowing you will have the privilege of making a diorama about *Little House on the Prairie* ever encouraged anyone to do the reading itself.

What is so important in this sixth precept is what Blake (1979) calls the sense of responsibility and feeling of trust that are engendered. Surely few positive feelings about reading will develop if the students perceive reading as something they have to be forced to do. And when the teacher makes them account for every book, then they will perceive reading as something that must not be inherently valuable; otherwise; the teacher could trust them to do it without proof.

7. *The teacher trusts the children to decide when something is well written when something has been read (because the teacher expects pupils to share after* SSR*).* At first glance "expects," in the preceding quotation by McCracken and McCracken, may appear to contradict the idea of trust. What is really expected is that the child will seriously *consider* if there is something about the book worth sharing. Not every book is worth sharing and, therefore, the reader should have the option of not sharing. Even if the book is good, it should be the student's choice to share the book. In fact, Petre (1971) reports that secondary school students would actually force books on the teachers so they could talk to them about what they had read. But the initiative should remain with the student.

A good recreational reading program can help students develop many positive feelings about reading and about books. A reading program that ignores the importance of voluntary, sustained reading may result in students who view reading as something one does only when one is forced to and only for very short periods of time.

Expansion of Experiential Background

How sad it would be if all we "knew about the world" was based only on our own experiences. Few of us have ever met a real pirate; but because of our acquaintance with Long John Silver, Bluebeard, Jean Lafitte, and Captain Hook we "know" what some pirates must have been like. We have a glimmer of what war, slavery, and the lives of royalty are like. Anne Frank, Willie Loman, and even Charlotte have changed us in tiny ways and altered our views of the world. Of course, in the past 30 years, television has done much to add to our knowledge of the world. But for me, at least, books have done more. With a book, I can stop and savor the experience and expand upon it in my own imagination. Television just doesn't give me that time nor that freedom.

For students with restricted backgrounds, expanding worlds through books is especially important. Children who have never traveled beyond their neighborhood, who have never been in a barn and smelled the blend of hay and animals, who have never been jostled by noisy, impersonal crowds on city sidewalks, can begin the circuitous route toward expanding the worlds in their heads by reading. The route is circuitous because readers find it is difficult to comprehend something about which they know very little. And yet, through grappling with an unfamiliar topic and trying to impose some sort of order on the mass of new information, the reader absorbs some of this information. Each time the reader meets this topic, bits and pieces of knowledge from previous experiences aid in comprehension and more bits and pieces are added. As new information is added, old information may be reorganized. Eventually the reader begins to develop a schema or framework for understanding the topic or situation.

The idea that experiential background aids comprehension is not new to teachers. However, recent research in schema theory (e.g., Anderson, Reynolds, Schallert, and Goetz, 1977; Pickert and Anderson, 1977) has begun to demonstrate empirically the importance of well-organized knowledge about a topic to both interpretation and remembering. Without a framework into a topic to both interpretation and remembering. Without a framework into which new information can be slotted, comprehension is severely hampered.

No claim is being made here that schemata are built only through reading. *All* of one's experiences, whether they be real or vicarious, contribute to what one knows about the world. But reading can help children multiply those experiences and that knowledge immeasurably with little inconvenience. Furthermore, unlike film and television, children can select the time, the place, and the kind of experience. Children can control the pace of the input of the information and can interact with the information in personal ways that are not possible with films and television. Reading allows readers to grow at their own pace and in unique, individualized ways. Reading is personalized in a way that television and film can never be.

Practice in Decoding Strategies:
Development of Automaticity

Most (unfortunately, not all) teachers would agree that the ultimate goal of reading is understanding. Identifying the words is just a step on the way to this final goal. LaBerge and Samuels (1976) suggest that if too much attention is focused on identifying the words, then not enough attention will be left for focusing on the ideas. They hypothesize that the development of automaticity in word processing (i.e., the ability to identify words without attending to the process) is crucial for comprehension.

LaBerge and Samuels use as examples physical skills that require the automatic integration of several subskills into the larger, complex act. Think of learning to ride a bicycle (think of teaching your own child to ride if it's too far back to remember your own experience). Think of being able to ski or dance. The final fluid performance comes about by being able to do all of the little parts without even thinking. As soon as you start attending to which finger goes on the H or whether this hip goes out as that arm goes up, the performance is disrupted.

Now consider how you got to be a world champion skier or a Fred Astaire on the dance floor. You did it by practice. And practice and practice. You started off slowly and worked your way up to stardom.

Finally, think about how this all relates to recreational reading. You learn to be a fluent reader, a comprehender, by practice with reading that is easy for you. And you practice with reading that is enjoyable to you. If you don't practice, you won't get good at it; you won't develop the automaticity that allows you to focus your attention on the ideas and not the words.

Several implications for recreational reading can be derived from this discussion. First, the automaticity model points out the need for practice and a recreational reading program provides time for this practice within the school day. Children are not expected to do all of their practice reading outside of school. Mork (1972) points out that for years "the silent reading parts of basal reader lessons have been largely ignored. Silent reading practice for most children seems to have been placed in that category entitled: 'for-enrichment-if-extra-time-is available'" (p. 439). When a recreational reading program is in operation, students are given practice time in school because time for practice is seen as a valued part of the curriculum, not just as a "bonus" that may or may not take place.

Second, children should be allowed to practice on what is easy for them. Many teachers and parents want to challenge children and look upon easy reading as coddling them or letting them be lazy. There's a tinge of Puritanism in that argument that seems to be saying, "If it doesn't hurt, it's not worthwhile." And yet few of us picked up our skis on the second outing and ran the expert hill or immediately went from playing scales to Chopin. If we are to encourage recreational reading, we must allow children to pace themselves. An occasional nudge here and there to give up the security of the bunny slope would not be amiss but, for the most part, children should be allowed to judge what is right for them. McCracken (1971) has called sustained silent reading "the drill of silent reading." Too much challenge likely means less drill or practice and less practice can mean slower development of automaticity.

A third implication of this argument is that self-selection of content as well as difficulty is important. Children should be allowed to read something they *want* to read. As adults, we tend to do more of what we enjoy and if children are reading something personally enjoyable, they will practice more. Again, when children read only books about motorcycles or ballet, some cajoling hints may be in order. But, in order to foster a maximum amount of easy, enjoyable practice, the final decision should be the children's.

Development of the Use of Context Clues

One of the most important strategies for word identification is the use of context clues. Most reading programs incorporate instruction in context clues into their lessons and provide opportunities for guided practice through workbooks and duplicated worksheets. More than this is needed, however, if children are to become spontaneous users of context clues. After instruction and guided practice, developing readers need opportunities to recognize and utilize context clues on their own, without supervision and without a set to "use the context to help you figure out the words you don't know." Recreational reading provides those opportunities.

Recreational reading has three qualities that should help to ensure that children do use context clues successfully to identify unknown words. First, because the reading material is self-selected, the children *want* to understand what is read. They will be predisposed to use context clues (or any other available strategy) to gain meaning because they are reading by choice, not by force. The use of context clues will be practiced in a natural, relevant setting rather than in the sterile, drill-like setting of worksheets and workbooks, during which young readers use context clues only to satisfy someone else.

Second, because the reading material is self-selected, chances are that the children can actually read the material. Of course, many children will occasionally choose a book that is at their frustration level (that is, that they cannot decode with more than 90 percent accuracy and more than 50 percent comprehension). However, more often students will read something at their independent or instructional levels.* For that reason, children will be able to read enough of the context to be able to use the context clues. If you can't read the words around the unknown word, you can't use those words to help identify the troublesome word.

Third, recreational reading is a "natural" for developing the use of context clues. For context clues to be useful, readers have to be able to derive meaning from the context. Readers who do not know what a "nog" is don't find "He slipped the nogs into the bricks" particularly illuminating. But young readers who choose books for leisure reading are likely to select books about topics or themes or with characters that are somewhat familiar rather than books about totally unknown subjects. And because the readers have some idea of what is going on or is being discussed, many of the context clues will be meaningful.

These characteristics that make recreational reading useful for developing context clues have an important procedural implication. If children are reading books they want to read, that are easy to read, and that are somewhat familiar, then teachers should be wary of interfering with the self-selection process. Before pushing a book on a reluctant student, the teacher should conscientiously determine if it destroys any of the characteristics discussed above. If so, perhaps self-selection should prevail.

Development of a Meaning Vocabulary

Reflect for a moment on how *you* learn new words. Most likely you learn many new words by listening to others—to your friends and to individuals on television and radio. You also learn new words through your professional reading. But a large proportion of your ever-increasing meaning vocabulary (that is, the words for which you have at least one meaning, whether you recognize the visual form of the word or not) comes from meeting

---

*The criteria for independent level are 99 percent decoding accuracy and 90 percent comprehension. The criteria for instructional level are 95 percent decoding accuracy and 75 percent comprehension (Betts, 1946).

words in print while doing recreational reading. No one taught you these words. You didn't have to find a definition for each word in the dictionary and then use it in one meaningful sentence. (Sure, you remember having to *do* that, but did you honestly learn many words that way?) You learned the meanings by meeting the words again and again in a variety of contexts in which you were usually able to figure out the meanings. Eventually you didn't *need* to figure out some of the words. You *knew* them. They were yours.

The development of a wide meaning vocabulary is essential for successful reading. The more words and meanings readers have in their heads, the more fluent the reading will be. All of us have listened to readers laboriously identify correctly the pronunciation of a word in context, only to watch with sinking heart as readers reject that pronunciation because it doesn't sound like a word they know. On the other hand, we have all heard readers arrive at an incorrect pronunciation of a word in context and then seen the flash of triumph as they quickly reject the distorted pronunciation for the real one. That quick "kick-in" of the real word could not happen if the word were not already somewhere in the reader's meaning vocabulary.

Teachers cannot hope to teach directly all the words they want their students to know. They can hope to teach a few words through carefully designed vocabulary development programs. They can also aspire to stimulate enthusiasm for words in their students so that the youngsters will seek out new words and take pride in learning to use these new words with precision and effect. They can teach the children how to use context clues to arrive at meanings for words.

Recreational reading provides the opportunities for meeting new words in contexts to which readers can apply the strategies and enthusiasm the teacher has taught. Sometimes, of course, the word is not important enought to stop and figure out the meaning ("Her puce sweater was lovely."); sometimes the word is so well-defined in context that the reader is almost unconscious of meeting a new word ("The puce color of her sweater was so dark a red that it almost appeared burgundy."). But sometimes the meaning of the word makes enough of a difference that the reader must determine a meaning for the word or fail in comprehending the text ("Caroline's puce sweater was decorated with tiny embroidered flowers. She admired Cecily's taupe sweater with its sparkling rhinestone buttons. Suddenly a shot exploded the quiet hum of the tearoom and the bright red of blood began to spread across the dark red of the girl's sweater.")

As the reader meets the word again and again, its meaning eventually becomes instantly recognized. But without wide reading the learner may not get enough practice with the word to make it truly known. "Once is not enough" for vocabulary development.

In Conclusion

Although a good recreational reading program is not likely to cure your warts nor bring you fame and fortune, in many respects it may be the answer to a teacher's prayer. It's easy. It's inexpensive. It's relatively painless. And most important of all, anyone can participate, because it starts where children are in reading and then helps children to get better. How could you pass up a bargain like that!

RESEARCH ON RECREATIONAL READING

On the preceding pages several arguments have been presented for including a recreational reading component in any developmental reading program. Many benefits from such a program have been described. And yet there is very little empirical evidence to back up the claims that recreational reading really does have positive effects on children's reading achievements or attitudes toward reading. It's not that there has been a great deal of research to show that recreational reading *doesn't* have positive effects; it's just that there hasn't been much "hard" research in this area at all.

Towner and Evans (1975) identified one of the most salient problems in proving that recreational reading programs really do help children read more and better. Concentrating on the SSR aspect of recreational reading, these authors pointed out that most of the claims that SSR improves attitude, increases attention span, leads to better reading, and so on are based primarily on the subjective judgments of those involved. Rather than relying on carefully designed studies which compare recreational reading with other procedures, proponents of recreational reading have chosen in many cases to support their claims by such subjective data as: "1) the increased popularity of SSR; 2) positive comments from students who have experienced

SSR; 3) positive comments from teachers who have used SSR; and 4) authoritative proclamation" (p. 84). The overwhelming conclusions from reports of this type are that both teachers and students like recreational reading programs and that teachers feel certain the students have derived many benefits from these programs.

However much our own good intuition and knowledge about reading leads us to believe in recreational reading, most of us would be a lot happier if there were some hard data to support these beliefs. Some such data do exist. A recent report by the Philadelphia school system (Kean, Summers, Raivetz, and Farber, 1979) showed that spending more time with independent reading led to significantly higher reading achievement scores for fourth grade students. Cohen (1968) found that low SES second grade students whose teachers read to them one story a day from a prescribed list and who completed follow-up activities had significantly greater comprehension and vocabulary gains than the students in the control group. In an Australian study, Connor (1954) found a strong relationship between voluntary reading and reading achievement of twelve year olds, if intelligence were held constant. In a two-year study of a supplementary recreational reading program, Pfau (1966) found the experimental group to be significantly superior in sight vocabulary and on a measure of written language fluency. However, there were no significant differences in comprehension or word analysis measures. Langford (1978) found that fifth and sixth graders who had engaged in an SSR program for six months had more positive attitudes toward reading on one of three attitude measures and performed significantly higher on the Slosson Oral Reading Test than did the control group.

A few other studies have failed to find significant effects on reading achievement but have found positive effects on other variables. For example, Wilmot (1975) found better attitudes toward reading by the experimental group (although the control group scored significantly better on the comprehension measure). However, many of these studies also relied on such "soft" signs as number of books checked out of the library and more reading activity to support conclusions that recreational reading has benefits. Although much of this "soft" evidence is impressive (such as Roberts' 1977 report that 2,350 children checked out 82,509 books in 3 months), such data sources do not carry the weight needed to convince many of the value of recreational reading.

Other studies have found no significant differences between groups engaged in recreational reading programs and groups engaged in other activities. Evans and Towner (1975) compared reading achievement of students using SSR to that of students using commercially produced practice materials such as those prepared by Barnell Loft and *Reader's Digest.* The investigators found no significant differences between the two groups on the Metropolitan Achievement Test. Reed (1977) found that secondary school students who had one period of SSR a week for five and one-half months did not score significantly differently on reading comprehension and attitude measures than students who followed the traditional curriculum. Bissett (1969) examined the effect of the number of books reported read on vocabulary and reading comprehension scores. He did not find significant effects on these variables. Oliver (1973, 1976) found that intermediate students engaged in High Intensity Practice (periods combining SSR, sustained silent writing, and self-selected activities involving active response to words) did not perform significantly better on measures of speed and accuracy, vocabulary, or comprehension. Mikulecky and Wolf (1977) investigated the declining attitude of seventh graders' toward reading. They found that students involved in SSR had the least loss in attitude over a 10-week period of the three treatment groups in the study (SSR, Self-Selected Reading Games, and Self-Selected Reading Skills). However, the SSR students did show decline in their attitudes and the differences among the three groups were not significant.

Moore, Jones, and Miller (1980) completed a comprehensive view of research in recreational reading. They suggested that although few studies have been done in the field, two conclusions may be supported from those studies: 1) "SSR has a positive effect on student attitude toward reading" and 2) "SSR has a positive effect on reading ability when combined with a regular program of reading instruction" (p. 448). Whereas Towner and Evans criticized the lack of rigorous research on recreational reading, Moore, Jones, and Miller pointed out some of the reasons why research that *has* been done may have failed to show more positive effects. One problem, also identified by Mork (1972), may be that researchers are attempting to measure changes over too short a time span. The primary goal of recreational reading, as identified in this monograph, is the development of children who choose to read. That is, recreational reading programs are designed primarily to inculcate the *habit* of reading. And habits are not developed in one- or two-month programs. Hopefully, more long term studies will show that over time students in recreational reading programs do develop differently from students who are denied such programs.

Moore, Jones, and Miller suggest that another reason for the lack of significant differences is the failure to select appropriate variables and reliable instruments for measuring these variables. They agree with Coughlin (1977) that variables other than reading test scores might be appropriate indexes of the value of recreational reading. Oliver (1976), for example, suggests that the ability to sustain oneself in silent reading might be an appropriate variable. Many of the enthusiastic reports about recreational reading programs do mention other variables as having been positively affected; but most of these reports have not measured these effects in any systematic, objective way. Reliable, valid instruments need to be developed to measure these variables.

Whaley (1980) recommends a six-step procedure that should greatly enhance research in recreational reading. Since many of the reports of recreational reading have their origins in the public schools, rather than in the universities, Whaley suggests ways in which classroom teachers can help to gather convincing data on the value of such programs:

1. Make a list of *all* the broad goals you aim to achieve at least partially through your recreational reading program.
2. Turn the list of goal statements into a list of questions.

3. For each question, list some alternative answers you might find.
4. Consider *all* the possible methods you can think of that would provide information to help answer the questions.... Then select at least two methods for each question. But select only the ones you think you can or will actually do. Don't overburden yourself.
5. Next plan when and how each evaluation method will be carried out and who will help you with each.
6. Once you have gathered the information, look at it collectively to see where different sources of information corroborate each other and use the results to answer your initial questions.

Whaley warns that determining if a program is good or bad is *not* the most important purpose of this data collection and evaluation. The most important purpose is to help the classroom teacher decide how to change and improve the program. But a valuable side benefit is that we may begin accumulating more objective data about the efficacy of recreational reading programs.

If the recommendations of Whaley and of Moore, Jones, and Miller are followed, I am convinced that research will validate what many of us intuitively feel is valuable about recreational reading programs. When such validation is found, reliance on subjective impressions will no longer be necessary. Furthermore, there may no longer need to be reliance on arguments to the effect that since recreational reading doesn't *harm* anyone and since it's less expensive, easier, and more fun than many of the traditional approaches, you might as well use it. At present both subjective impressions and negative arguments do carry some weight for those who want to believe in recreational reading anyway. But more evidence is needed, both to convince the skeptics and to make the proponents truly confident in their beliefs.

References

Allington, R. If they don't read much, how they ever gonna get good? *Journal of Reading,* 1977, *21*(1), 57-61.

Anderson, R.C., Reynolds, R.E., Schallert, D.L., & Goetz, E.T. Frameworks for comprehending discourse. *American Educational Research Journal,* 1977, *14*(4), 367-381.

Athey, I. Fashioning the will to read. *Reporting on Reading: Right to Read,* 1978, *4*(3), 1-2; 8.

Betts, E.A. *Foundations of reading instruction.* New York: American Book, 1946.

Bissett, D.J. The amount and effect of recreational reading in selected fifth grade classes. (Doctoral dissertation, Syracuse University, 1969.) *Dissertation Abstracts International,* 1969, *30,* 5157-A. (University Microfilms No. 7010316)

Blake, M.E. SSR revisited. *Teacher,* 1979, *96,* 95-98.

Cohen, D. The effect of literature on vocabulary and reading achievement. *Elementary English,* 1968, *45,* 209-213, 217.

Connor, D. The relationship between reading achievement and voluntary reading of children. *Educational Review,* 1954, *6,* 221-227.

Coughlin, A.G. SSR: The strand that untangles the skein. *Curriculum Review,* 1977, *16*(5), 352-353.

Gallup, G. *The Gallup poll: Public opinion, 1935-1971.* New York: Random House, 1972.

Greaney, V., & Quinn, J. Factors related to amount and type of leisure time reading. Paper presented at the Seventh IRA World Congress on Reading, Hamburg, Germany, 1978. (ED163402)

Hunt, L.C., Jr. The effect of self-selection, interest, and motivation upon independent, instructional, and frustrational levels. *Reading Teacher,* 1970, *24*(2), 146-151, 158.

Kean, M.H., Summers, A.A., Raivetz, M.J., & Farber, I.J. *What works in reading?* Philadelphia: The School District of Philadelphia, 1979.

LaBerge, D., & Samuels, S.J. Toward a theory of automatic information processing in reading. In H. Singer & R. Ruddell (Eds.), *Theoretical models and processes of reading,* second edition. Newark, Delaware: International Reading Association, 1976, 548-579.

Langford, J.C. The effects of uninterrupted sustained silent reading on the attitudes of students toward reading and their achievement in reading. (Doctoral dissertation, Auburn University, 1978.) *Dissertation Abstracts International,* 1979, *39,* 4047-A, 4047B. (University Microfilms No. 7900160)

LeGrand-Brodsky, K. Hope for reading in America: Practically everyone reads. *Reading Teacher,* 1979, *32*(8), 947-950.

Ley, T.C. Getting kids into books: The importance of individualized reading. *Media & Methods,* 1979, *15,* 22-24.

McCracken, R.A. Initiating sustained silent reading. *Journal of Reading,* 1971, *14*(8), 521-524, 582-583.

McCracken, R.A., & McCracken, M.J. Modeling is the key to sustained silent reading. *Reading Teacher,* 1978, *31*(4), 406-408.

Mikulecky, L., & Wolf, A. Effect of uninterrupted sustained silent reading and of reading games on changes in secondary students' reading attitudes. In P.D. Pearson (Ed.), *Reading: Theory, research and practice.* Twenty-sixth yearbook of the National Reading Conference. Clemson, S.C.: National Reading Conference, 1977, 126-130.

Moore, J.C., Jones, C.J., & Miller, D.C. What we know after a decade of sustained silent reading. *Reading Teacher*, 1980, *33*(4), 445-450.

Mork, T.A. Sustained silent reading in the classroom. *Reading Teacher*, 1972, *25*(5), 438-441.

Oliver, M.E. The effect of high intensity practice on reading achievement. *Reading Improvement*, 1976, *13*(4), 226-228.

Oliver, M.E. The effect of high intensity practice on reading comprehension. *Reading Improvement*, 1973, *10*, 16-18.

Petre, R.M. Reading breaks make it in Maryland. *Journal of Reading*, 1971, *15*(3), 191-194.

Pfau, D.W. An investigation of the effects of planned recreational reading programs in first and second grade. (Doctoral dissertation, State University of New York at Buffalo, 1966.) *Dissertation Abstracts International*, 1966, *27*, 1719-A. (University Microfilms No. 6613086)

Pichert, J.W., & Anderson, R.C. Taking different perspectives on a story. *Journal of Educational Psychology*, 1977, *69*, 309-315.

Reed, K. An investigation of the effect of sustained silent reading on reading comprehension skills and attitude toward reading of urban secondary school students. (Doctoral dissertation, University of Connecticut, 1977.) *Dissertation Abstracts International*, 1977, *38*, 4718-A. (University Microfilms No. 7731216)

Roberts, E.P. Reading up a storm. *Early Years*, 1977, *8*, 28-29, 58-59.

Towner, J.C., & Evans, H.M. The S.S. Reading: Does it float? *Reading Horizons*, 1975, *15*, 83-86.

Whaley, J. Discussant of D.L. Spiegel, Recreational reading (How not to go berserk). Paper presented at the International Reading Association Annual Convention, St. Louis, May 1980.

Wilmot, M.P. An investigation of the effect upon the reading performance and attitude toward reading of elementary grade students, of including in the reading program a period of sustained, silent reading. (Doctoral dissertation, University of Colorado, 1975.) *Dissertation Abstracts International*, 1976, *36*, 5029-A, 5030-A. (University Microfilms No. 763968)

Yankelovich, Skelly & White, Inc. *The 1978 consumer research study on reading and book purchasing.* BISG Report No. 6, Book Industry Study Group, 1978.

PRACTICE

MOTIVATING STUDENTS TO READ FOR PLEASURE

The basic idea of a recreational reading program is very simple: Let kids read. Experienced teachers, however, would respond with a great big "Ha!" if anyone were to suggest that implementing such a simple idea is a snap. Some children don't want to read. Others will read certain kinds of material to the exclusion of all others. Administrators or parents may be reluctant to let students spend potential instructional time just reading. Questions of accountability must be resolved. Materials must be gathered and organized. Yet in spite of these potential problems, the development and maintenance of a successful recreational reading program is possible and can be a lot of fun.

If the goal of any recreational reading program is to produce students who choose reading over other activities, then it seems reasonable to assume that motivation would be of primary importance to such a program. Unless the students are motivated to read on their own, *because they want to*, the program will not be a success, regardless of the number of books read as a result of prodding by the teacher. True, prodding, cajolery, bribery, and just plain nagging may be necessary to get a recreational reading program off the ground. Progress may be slow at first. A very structured program, such as sustained silent reading, may be needed at the beginning. But if after several months students still read only when prodded or only during the ssr period, then the recreational reading program is a flop.

Motivation for recreational reading often begins with teachers. They are the ones who introduce the idea, initiate the program, find time for student reading during the busy day and, in general, "sell" books and reading. Motivation may move from the teachers to the students as members of groups. That is, the students are beginning to enjoy reading for itself, but a primary reason for reading is to experience the group interaction that results from reading the same book or from sharing reading with interested others. Eventually, the motivation should move from other-direction to inner-direction. That is, individuals enjoy reading for itself, because it satisfies personal needs. Students may still enjoy interacting with others about books and may still like pleasing the teacher by reading, but the main force driving children toward reading is love of reading. That should be the end result of a recreational reading program.

Teacher Attitudes

Think about the subject you have *least* enjoyed teaching. Now think about how your students felt about that subject. Did they learn to share your lack of enthusiasm? Consider how often you actually got around to teaching that subject. Was it often the first one to be scrapped when an assembly program was squeezed into your already busy day? Was it the subject you scheduled for last period and, as a result, occasionally didn't teach? All this introspection leads to what I believe is the most important factor in any recreational reading program: The teacher really has to believe in the value of the program.

This overwhelming faith in the inherent value of recreational reading is essential for at least four reasons. First of all, you can't "sell" something you don't believe in yourself. Unless teachers like to read and can communicate this joy to their students, they may have trouble convincing the children that reading is something they will enjoy, too. Even five year olds can spot a con job pretty quickly (Santa Claus notwithstanding) and forced enthusiasm will plant seeds of suspicion. Recreational reading has to look like something enticing and wonderful and fun, and a ho-hum attitude by the teacher is not likely to entice anyone.

A second reason the teacher must really believe in recreational reading is guilt. Of course, a few teachers think nothing of taking potential instructional time to finish a crocheting project or to work on a paper for a graduate class. But most teachers feel that the major portions of their days should be spent interacting with children, whether in small or large groups or with individuals. Such teachers eagerly seize moments when most of the class are working independently to draw individuals aside for extra help and encouragement. They find it difficult to sit back and model recreational reading by reading themselves. They also find it disturbing to ignore these spontaneous instructional opportunities and just let the children read.

McCracken and McCracken (1978) informally examined SSR programs that seemed to be floundering. In the majority of these unsuccessful programs, they found teachers who were, for whatever reasons, reluctant to join the children in recreational reading. As the McCrackens pointed out, if the teacher or the aide is doing something other than reading, some children will prefer watching that activity (regardless of how dull it is) to reading. Teachers must believe that their time modeling silent reading is well spent.

Other teachers have similar feelings about the children's use of time. Every year some curriculum expert adds something new that second graders are supposed to learn before third grade. Accountability and the accompanying standardized testing always lurks nearby. The thought of "wasting" precious minutes of class time by just letting children read causes tremendous pangs of guilt for some of these teachers. And yet for all the reasons mentioned in the first part of this book, recreational reading *is* worth the time. Giving children time to read *is* doing your job.

A third reason for the belief in the program is that teachers may need to convince administrators and parents that recreational reading is important enough to warrant class time. These adults may have the same qualms about use of teacher and student time that cause guilt twinges in the teachers. In order to

Practice

convince administrators and parents that recreational reading outside the classroom is not enough, teachers must be convinced themselves.

In the fourth place, unless teachers are really committed to recreational reading, they may find the time for reading "slip-sliding away." Teachers must find time for discussing Fire Prevention or making posters for The Fight Against Tooth Decay or other special interests that seep into the school day in addition to the basic curriculum. Unless recreational reading is deemed as important as math or spelling, it may be the first activity to give way to these temporary demands.

Furthermore, if recreational reading is perceived as a frill by the teacher, it will be scheduled accordingly into children's daily lives. Recreational reading will be the thing you do when all the rest of your work is done. And that means that some children will *never* get to do recreational reading because they never finish their assigned work.

Many ways exist for teachers to show students, parents, and administrators how much they value reading and the recreational reading program. Brutten (1974) asked middle school students to respond to the following questions: What has a teacher of yours done to interest you in reading? What could a teacher of yours do to interest you in reading? Six of the top 25 responses directly related to teachers' piquing student interest in specific books by: Telling interesting stories, showing film-strips or films about stories, suggesting names of interesting stories, playing records that tell stories, telling only the beginning of interesting stories, and preparing teacher and/or student annotated book lists (p. 74). These responses seem to indicate that the students did not really feel confident in their own abilities to find "good" books, that they would welcome suggestions.

One of the best ways to introduce students (or adults) to new books is to read aloud to them, either entire books or just interesting portions of books. Classroom teachers of all ages know that it's not only music that hath charms to sooth the savage breast, but also a good story. All the work is being done by the readers; the listeners can just relax and enjoy the story. As a result, children may learn to associate reading with pleasure. Furthermore, teachers are showing the audience that reading is something they enjoy and value. This is especially important at the beginning of a recreational reading program when some individuals may not yet be convinced that sitting down with a book could be of any interest.

Many teachers are unsure whether a particular book will be interesting to their students. To combat this, one San Antonio, Texas, school district established a coordinated district-wide program for reading aloud to students (Faller, 1978). Twenty-two volunteer schools each sent a 3-member team consisting of a classroom teacher, a librarian, and a principal to an organizational meeting. These team members developed a reporting system whereby any person in the 22 schools who read a book to children could fill out a review card. On the review card the reader would include a summary of the book, a rating, any comments about the book's unique characteristics or value, and recommendations for appropriate grade levels. No card was to be turned in unless the book had actually been read aloud to children. The cards were cross indexed and teachers used this index to help them select books to read to their students. Not unexpectedly, an important side effect of this program has been that the children themselves are now reading more.

A second way a teacher can show that recreational reading is valuable is simply to let the children talk about what they have read. In response to Brutten's questionnaire, the students were less than enthusiastic about book reports, but they did suggest that group and panel discussions about books would be of value. They also asked to be allowed "to tell the class about exciting books that we have read" (p. 63).

A third way for proving that recreational reading is important has already been mentioned: Give a regular and sufficient amount of time for recreational reading during every day. If something is important, time can be found to do it.

Rosler (1979) reports an exciting way in which an entire school showed how important reading is. The librarian prepared lessons that described the benefits of reading, showed books to children, and helped teachers set up their own classroom libraries. Science, music, and math teachers involved students in reading by suggesting "biographies, research topics, and books of puzzles, brainteasers, and problems to their pupils" (p. 397). The art teacher gave class time to the preparation of posters by the children to advertise the reading campaign. In addition, the teacher sponsored a schoolwide contest to design an official school bookmark. Then the industrial arts teacher supervised helpers while they made one bookmark for each child in the school. The student government advisor made sure that all students leaders were involved. The family programer and the PTA representatives informed parents about the program and worked hard to enlist their support. They even had books in the school's Family Room for parents to borrow. Undoubtedly, the children got the message that reading is important to *everyone*.

Grouping Procedures

Although teacher attitude is crucial for both initiating and maintaining a flourishing recreational reading program, such a program cannot be sustained if motivation comes exclusively from the teacher. Eventually, the motivation must come from within the individual. An important intermediate point between the initial impetus from the teacher's enthusiasm and the individual's final inner-directed desire to read may be the motivation that comes about from being a group member. At first the reading itself may be of less importance to the student than the social interaction that takes place within the group. The opportunity to work with the group, which comes about because of reading, may be the primary motivation. However, one would hope and expect that this enthusiasm would eventually transfer to reading itself as the group member had more pleasurable experiences associated with reading.

A teacher who wishes to use grouping to encourage recreational reading has a large variety of grouping procedures from which to choose. In fact, a teacher would be wise to employ a variety of procedures rather than to select just one. Some evidence exists (Kean, Summers, Raivetz, and Farber, 1979) that children whose teachers use varied grouping patterns achieve more in reading than children whose teachers use only one kind of group (regardless of the size of the group). Furthermore, if there are several choices of group sizes and interaction patterns, most children will be able to find the kind of group in which they are personally most comfortable.

Groups designed to foster recreational reading may vary in size from pairs to entire classrooms. In this discussion of grouping, however, I will not deal with the classroom as a group because the interaction in a group of 25-35 does not have the quality that comes about in a group of 2-8.

Small groups of 4-8 readers may be formed in several ways within a single classroom or even across classrooms. These groups can be based on common topics such as dinosaurs, famous inventors, or sports stories or on common genre such as poetry, plays, comic books, or magazines. The group may also be formed without regard to what is being read but with emphasis on the composition of the group itself. Children may be allowed to form a temporary group of their special friends. Teachers may make up a group designed to improve class relationships and to get interaction among children who rarely talk with each other. Occasionally, totally arbitrary groups may be formed—all the students who have on blue today form a group—just to spice things up.

Yatvin (1977) reports on a schoolwide grouping pattern that was quite successful. Each member of the professional staff in the entire school was responsible for working with a small group of children for the 30 minutes immediately after lunch each day. The student body was polled to determine their favorite reading-related activities and the 6 most popular activities were used to form 13 recreational reading groups. For example, in one of these groups children listened to an adult read poetry; in some groups the children themselves read aloud; in other groups all the members read silently. Play-reading was a popular activity, whereas the reading of comic books was eventually phased out due to lack of interest. Before the children signed up for specific 4-week groups, each teacher who would be reading aloud to a group would post a list of the specific material to be heard. However, in order to keep the signing-up process from being a popularity contest, the students were not aware of which teacher sponsored which group.

Thus every child was involved in recreational reading in some form each day, but the child was not limited only to the form selected by the classroom teacher. Every 4 weeks new groups were established and new kinds of recreational reading were available.

Another grouping pattern that would lend itself easily to recreational reading is jigsaw grouping (Aronson, Blaney, Sikes, Stephan, and Snapp, 1975). In jigsaw grouping, each individual is a member of two groups. For recreational reading, the first set of groups might be based on interest. One group would read about spiders (I-A), one about sports records (I-B), one about recording stars, (I-C), and one about China (I-D). Each member of each interest group would read independently for several days to gather information about the chosen topic. Then the interest group would meet together to pool information and to develop a group outline of important information.

After each interest group had written an outline of information to share, new groups would be formed in the following manner: Group II-A would consist of one person from the spider group, one from the sports records group, one from recording stars group, and one from the China group. All the other Group IIs would have the same mix. Then within each Group II every member would share the information learned as a member of Group I. As a result, each person in the class would gain some new information about spiders, sports records, recording stars, and China and each person would get a chance to be the "teacher" within his or her Group II. In addition, children who seem to get stuck on just one topic ("But I'm not interested in anything but auto racing!") will at least have to listen to other kinds of information that can be gleaned from reading.

Jigsaw grouping would be particularly valuable when a teacher felt that certain students remained outside the mainstream of classroom interactions. Aronson et al. (1975) found that this pattern of grouping improved race relations within a classroom. This improvement was most likely based on two

Jigsaw Grouping

Group I-A (spiders)	Group I-B (sports records)	Group I-C (recording stars)	Group I-D (China)
Diane	Walter	Bill	Ann
Scott	Marie	Mike	Marlene
Carlos	Sam	Alice	Bob
Debbie	Jane	John	Travis

Group II-A	Group II-B	Group II-C	Group II-D
Diane (spiders)	Scott	Carlos	Debbie
Walter (sports records)	Marie	Sam	Jane
Bill (recording stars)	Mike	Alice	John
Ann (China)	Marlene	Bob	Travis

causes. 1) Students of different races simply did not interact often enough to learn to value members of the other race. Jigsaw-grouping forced this interaction. 2) Within the structure of jigsaw grouping students *had* to pay attention to all members of their group because each member had unique information for which all members would be held responsible. Although using jigsaw grouping for recreational reading purposes would tend to eliminate Reason 2 (in part), all students would still be responsible for listening to the others if they wanted the others to listen to *them*.

One very simple grouping pattern is that of pairs or "reading buddies." Roeder and Lee (1973) suggest that each child choose a temporary partner and at specific times the partners read aloud to each other. The pairs concept could be extended in several ways. The pair could read silently about the same topic and could share information with each other; they could read about entirely different topics and share. They could read the same book and jointly prepare a report for the class designed to "sell" that book. They could read different books and try to sell to each other. Partners basically would be individuals with whom readers could share when and if they wanted to.

Grouping for recreational reading can easily be accomplished within a basal reader program. Smith and Johnson

(1976, pp. 52-64) suggest that each student be a member of three groups. In the skill-development group students of approximately the same reading ability and skill needs meet for comprehension and word identification instruction, with the basal reader forming the focus of this instruction. The skill-development group is a relatively stable one, although often only certain members will receive instruction in a particular skill and individualized assignments will be common.

Each student is also a member of a recreational reading group. Unlike the skill-development groups, each recreational reading group is made up of students with varied reading abilities, with children reading self-selected material at their own pace. After the group has read silently (Smith and Johnson recommend they do this in a small circle), the children share with one another what they have just been reading. From time to time the composition of these groups is changed.

The third group is the information-getting group. These groups, too, are heterogeneous in regard to reading ability. However, all members of the group share an interest in a common topic. These students meet together for two or three weeks to gather information about this topic and to prepare a group presentation for the class. Then new groups are formed based on different interests.

To see how the teacher can juggle all three kinds of groups, let us consider six children. A-1 and A-2 are above average readers; B-1 and B-2 are average; and C-1 and C-2 are poor readers. A two-day schedule for these six individuals for a one-and-one-half hour reading class might look like the illustration on page 36.

Sustained silent reading (SSR) may be an excellent way of providing time for recreational reading. But combining children into interactive groups of various sizes and for varying reading-related purposes can help stimulate the interest in reading that is necessary for SSR to be successful. Children should have at all times several options for doing recreational reading. Having a variety of grouping patterns available (including the individual as a group in SSR) can provide these options.

Time	SKILL-DEVELOPMENT (teacher-directed, with independent follow up)	INFORMATION-GETTING (independent)	RECREATIONAL READING (independent)
9-9:20	B-1 & B-2	A-1 & C-2	A-2 & C-1
9:20-9:45		A-1, C-2, & B-2 A-2, C-1, & B-1	
9:45-10	C-1 & C-2		A-2 & B-1 A-1 & B-2
10-10:10	C-1		A-2, B-1, & C-2 A-1 & B-2
10:10-10:30	A-1 & A-2	C-1 & B-1 B-2	C-2
9-9:10	A-1	C-2 & B-2 B-1	A-2 & C-1
9:10-9:20	C-2	B-1 & C-1	A-1 & B-2 A-2
9:20-9:45	B-1 & B-2	A-1 A-2 & C-1	C-2
9:45-10:10	C-1 & C-2	A-1 & B-2 A-2 & B-1	
10:10-10:30	A-1 & A-2	C-2	B-1 B-2 & C-1

(Note that each group is not comprised of just these six individuals. For example, at 9:20 on day 2, C-2 would not be the only member of his or her recreational reading group reading at that time.)

Expanding Reading Interests

Helping children to expand their reading interests within a recreational reading program involves two distinct, sequential issues. First, one has to deal with the decision of whether it is even appropriate to utilize a recreational reading program as a means of broadening students' reading interests. Then, if one decides that in some ways it *is* appropriate, procedures for encouraging diverse reading can be explored.

The Appropriateness of Using a Recreational Reading Program to Expand Interests

One of the major principles of many recreational reading programs is that of self-selection. Teachers need to decide if their goal is relatively simple, to produce children who choose to read, or if their goal is to produce well-rounded readers. If teachers are satisfied with students who enjoy reading *something*, then allowing children to read whatever they wish is appropriate. However, many teachers feel a responsibility for guiding students toward good literature and for helping children to sample from the wide variety of reading material available.

Teachers with that point of view most likely will not allow their students free rein in selecting reading matter.

This section on expanding interests is written from a definite stance: The primary goal of a recreational reading program is to develop children who *will* read. If, in addition to this, teachers wish to help their students to develop broader reading interests, then low-key encouragement toward diversity in reading may be given. But children in a recreational reading program should never be forced to abandon self-selection in favor of what someone else thinks they "ought" to read. As Rathbun (1977) puts it, "The first priority is to get them to read; after that you and they and future teachers can work on *what* they should read" (p. 128).

In several studies in which children were asked how teachers could help them learn to enjoy reading, the responses were strongly in favor of "letting us choose our own books" (e.g., Brutten, 1974, and Heathington, 1979). Logic and our own experiences as adults support their position. Most of us don't mind an occasional helpful suggestion for a different or better way to do something, especially if we are novices at the activity. But we soon learn to avoid activities if teachers hover nearby insisting that we do it their way. Teachers who persist in forcing specific books on individual students run the risk of having the children associate reading with unpleasantness and nagging. If one goal for a recreational reading program is to assist children to choose reading material wisely, then teachers who insist on pushing their choices on the children are hampering this development.

Encouraging Children to Widen Their Reading Interests

Once children have learned to enjoy reading in some form, the teacher may wish to encourage them to explore other kinds of reading. Most of the suggestions that follow will be ways of exposing an entire classroom of children to interesting books, rather than procedures for urging a specific child to read a particular book. Concentrating on the whole class reduces the pressure any individual will feel and allows the encouragement of diversification to remain very low-key.

Identifying interests and using them to encourage diversity.
In order to broaden children's interests, you first have to know what their interests are. Many lists of children's reading interests have been compiled and several reading interest inventories are available for various age groups. Teachers may wish to consult these materials when gathering reading matter with which to entice their students. Information gathered through the administration of an interest inventory would give a teacher an idea of secondary interests of each student, even if the individual were still primarily enthralled with only one topic or genre. This information could form the basis upon which the gentle persuasion for expanding reading interests could begin.

A less complex way of matching child and book has been suggested by Indrisano (1978). She recommends that at the beginning of each month students be required to list one goal they each want to meet through reading. This goal might be to find out what happens to snakes in the winter or to learn more about Dr. Seuss or to read poetry about sports. The teacher then becomes involved as a resource person to assist each student in meeting this goal. To enforce diversity, the teacher could require that goals differ substantially from month to month. In this way, children are required to spend at least a small portion of their recreational reading time with matter that may not be of primary interest. However, the children are still selecting something of personal interest with a minimum of teacher interference. In addition, the children have ample time for completely free recreational reading.

Ley (1979) reports on another way of finding out about student reading interests. Class members are given book club order forms and each is allowed to "order" $5 worth of books. Then the teacher purchases the four or five most requested books.

In order to extend interests, a student might be permitted to select only one book in a single category. Thus an individual would be required to consider several kinds of reading material.

Another variation would be to form a committee each month (or however frequently books are ordered) to actually buy books for the classroom library. This committee would be made up of students of varied reading abilities and interests. Each committee member would be responsible for reviewing all of the books listed in the catalog and for helping to choose a broad selection.

A simple way of keeping track of who wants to read what is to have, in a permanent location, a folder in which students can jot down kinds of reading material they would like help in finding. When time permits, the teacher can either share the list with the librarian or assist the children personally in finding appropriate resources. The teacher could also gracefully decline to help a student find yet another book about trolls.

Criscuolo (1977) has borrowed the computerized dating format to involve the students themselves in finding books of interest to their classmates. Each child could fill out an "application" blank such as the one below:

Name _____
Hobbies _____
Favorite TV Program _____
Last Book I Read _____
Types of Books I Like _____
Age _____

These applications could then be posted or kept in an easily accessible file. Students who read or find books they think might be of interest to a classmate could tell about the book and where to find it or give the book to the individual. Through this "computerized matching" the children would be exposed to a variety of reading materials by their peers and not through the sometimes none-too-subtle ministrations of their teachers. Furthermore, even though this system has as its basis matching an individual with a book on an expressed interest, the interpretation by classmates of what will be interesting may be quite broad and, as a result, students may find their reading interests expanding.

Talking about books. One of the most effective ways of exposing children to varied reading materials is for teachers to talk about books and to let students know they enjoy reading certain books. Higgins and Kellman (1979) suggest that elementary grade students are more strongly influenced by teacher suggestions than are older students. Roettger (1980) interviewed students in grades 4-6 about how they would help children learn to enjoy reading if they were the teacher. The students reported that "teachers should tell children about interesting books and help them build pictures in their minds about what was happening" (p. 453). Teachers should take advantage of this suggestibility by "soft-selling" books as often as possible.

Usova (1978) mentions one of the easiest ways of "pushing" specific books: Teachers should put paperback books on their desks. The books may be ones the teachers have just finished reading or ones thought to be of interest to some of the students. Hopefully, someone will soon ask to borrow a book and it can be replaced with a book of a different kind.

Book Look Lunches (Hunter, 1980) are another way to get adults and children together to talk about what they've read. The principal, assistant principal, librarian, and reading specialist would each lunch as often as possible with different classes. Before eating with a particular student, the adult would review the record of books the child had read recently. At the lunch the adult and the child would discuss these books and the adult could make suggestions about other books the child might enjoy. Because these adults are such "special" people, the students might be more willing to follow their suggestions than those of the regular classroom teacher.

Of course, children also enjoy talking about books with their peers. Lamme (1976) found that recommendations by friends gained in importance as students grew older. Jigsaw grouping, as described previously, is an excellent way of getting children together to learn about different books. Having students do book talks over the school intercom or write book blurbs for the school newspaper also will introduce children to books of many different varieties (Ross, 1978).

The desire to be "in the know" about books can be a powerful motivator. Criscuolo (1977) suggests that students nominate their favorite books for Academy Awards. The top ten nominations would be voted on by the entire class. This idea could be extended to encourage diversity by having nominations by category. The top five books in each category could be made available for one or two months for easy student access. A student would read all or nearly all of the books in a single category in order to be eligible to vote for that category. If the student did not read at least 80 percent of the books in a category, that student could not help rank that category.

Talking with authors can spark children's interest in different books (Rathbun, 1977; Kraus and Haas, 1977). One school district compiled a list of authors who lived within a reasonable distance and periodically invited one of the authors to visit the schools and talk with the children (Faller, 1978). Librarians could cooperate by having special displays of the visiting author's work available a month or two ahead of the visit.

Abrahamsen (1977) recommends having children learn about authors as people as a way of enticing youngsters to broaden their reading. The students could write to the authors or read biographies about them. The same research could be done for illustrators. The personal element that comes about through talking with authors or learning about them may be just enough to pique an individual's interest in a new area or genre.

Advertising books and ideas. Sometimes teachers need to become advertising executives. They must know how to display their merchandise (in this case, books) to make it irresistible to the most blasé consumer. The display could be visual or verbal. But regardless of the format, the goal is to get the consumer to "bite."

Teachers may wish to develop units about a genre their students seem to be ignoring. For example, to introduce a class to the delights of folktales, a teacher might prepare a display of books of folktales. Then the teacher could read one folktale each day to the class, selecting a different nation of origin each time. As a final enticement, one folktale could be read in several different versions so the listeners could begin to understand the way many folktales are shared among nations.

Eisenberg and Notowitz (1979) described booktalks which were effective at the secondary level for extending student reading interests. These booktalks could be prepared by librarians, reading specialists, paraprofessionals, or volunteers and presented to several classrooms. Classroom teachers could develop booktalks for their own students. Some librarians may be willing to gather resource materials for classroom teachers to give their own booktalks. Then several teachers could use the same unit at different times and varied units would be available to teachers throughout the year. Classroom teachers could also trade visits with one another's classrooms.

A booktalk might be prepared on a theme or on a genre. The talk should take 20-30 minutes and should introduce the students to about 15 related books. To prepare for the talk, the presenter should read a biography of the author, any available reviews in trade journals, the book jackets, chapter headings, and selected portions of the book. During the talk itself a summary should be given of each book, plus any particularly intriguing tidbits about the author and any aspects about the plot or content that might be especially interesting or unusual. After a book has been discussed it should be passed around the class. The presenter should have several copies of each book. All books should be available for immediate checkout.

Cox (1980) has used a thematic approach for doing Shakespeare with intermediate age students. She reports great enthusiasm among the students for reading to find out how to create authentic costumes, props, and sets. Such a unit might easily be initiated by a booktalk to introduce the students to available resource materials and related works of fiction and poetry.

Teachers who feel their students need to explore the world of nonfiction more often might hold trivia contests (Stevens, 1980). Stevens' description is for fifth and sixth graders, but the format could easily be modified for younger students. Twenty-five topics (such as soccer, leprechauns, Argentina) could be chosen for the older children and four multiple-choice questions written for each topic. The topics and questions could be displayed on a bulletin board, at a learning center, or in a looseleaf notebook. As answers were found, they could be signed and dropped in an envelope. Individuals finding answers could write their names next to the questions. Stevens reports that often children would read an entire book after they had found the answer to a question, simply because they had become interested in the topic.

Another way to encourage students to vary their reading is to post a World of Books (Pelletier, 1979). The World of Books is a display made up of a large world map and a selection of books with many different settings. A construction paper arrow with the name of a book is placed on the map on the locale of that book. Since many books are set in an imaginary or unidentified setting, an eighth continent can be added to the map to provide a setting for these books. If the teacher wishes to have a record of what each child reads, a ticket can be made such as the one below. The ticket can be punched upon arrival and departure in order to provide interim reinforcement for the young reader.

Passenger _____

Flight Schedule	*Arrival Date*	*Departure Date*
(book name)	(date finished)	(date follow-up activity finished)

To develop interest in a specific book, Williams (1977) recommends placing the book in a cloth bag on a bulletin board. Next to the bag, place a piece of tagboard labeled *Questions and Answers*. The children write questions about the book on the tagboard and the teacher fills in the answers when the students are not around. Toward the end of the Mystery Book Bag period, a sign-up sheet could be put on the board for students who wanted to read the mystery book.

Just displaying books attractively may be enough to draw a child toward a different book. Some teachers buy or borrow used card display racks (both rotating and fixed varieties), and use them to hold their classroom libraries and to make books easily accessible and visible to their students.

Rewarding, recording, and researching. Gentle persuasion and multimedia displays may not be enough to get some children to abandon their comfortable cocoon of mystery books, sports stories, or dinosaur dramas. If the teacher feels very strongly that the child *must* branch out, a system of differential rewards may cause a breakthrough. Such a reward system may be tied to tangible rewards involving the entire class or may be a part of the fulfillment of routine class requirements. As an example of the latter system, some teachers may require an individual to read 6 books a grading period. To enforce diversity, the teacher may choose to give Sally 2 credits for every nonmystery book she reads and 1 credit for every mystery — Sally is addicted to mysteries. (A less positive system would give Sally only a half credit for each mystery book. I would prefer starting with the more positive approach.)

Similar differential rewards could be tied into procedures that offer tangible rewards for recreational reading. Flowers (1977) reports about a school that gave each child a helium filled balloon for every X books read. Inside each balloon the child could write a message requiring an answer, giving a return address. One answer came from the Netherlands! To encourage diversity in reading, the number of balloons received could be contingent upon the variety of books read, not just on the quantity.

Lough (1979) describes a procedure whereby students earned "money" from reading. The money was then used to bid at an auction of items sent by celebrities upon request by the class. The amount of money earned for each book was contingent upon the size of the book and the way in which follow-up activities were completed. Primary consideration, however, was given to the student's reading ability in order to ensure that each student had an equal opportunity to earn money. Each book was assigned to one of 24 categories and a $10 bonus was given if a student read a book in each category. To encourage less diversity, smaller bonuses might be given for reading in 5, 10, or 15 categories.

Recording class diversity in reading may encourage some children to expand into new areas. One teacher I know has taken pieces of colored tagboard and labeled each with a category she would like to encourage her students to sample. These pieces of tagboard are placed around the room and when children finish a book in that category, they write the name of the book and their name. In this way, the class can develop a sense of communal pride in having several books read in all categories. Furthermore, an individual who decides to read in a particular category can consult this class record as a quick way of finding the title of an appropriate book.

Some children may read books of the same type over and over because they know where to find those books easily and they don't know how to find other kinds. Brutten's students (1974) mentioned that it would help them become more interested in reading if the teacher would take them to the library. Similarly, Ross (1978) found that middle school students reported a need for lots of browsing time in the library, with personal assistance in finding particular books. Teachers who wish to expand their students' recreational reading interests need to be sure the students know how to find all kinds of reading material and have enough time in the library to make a thorough search for something new. Twenty minutes, once a week is inadequate.

Using a recreational reading program to broaden children's reading interests can be tricky. The teacher who makes the decision to do this should be very careful to keep the pressure for diversity very low-key and directed primarily toward the class as a whole and not toward specific individuals. The recreational reading program *can* be used in this way, but it should be done very cautiously.

Sharing Reading with Others

As with the question of expanding reading interests through recreational reading, the idea of sharing reading with others has two aspects: Should we and, if so, how?

Should we? I can think of no convincing argument for *requiring* children to share what they have read, either with the teacher or with other students. When I have made this comment to classroom teachers I have invariably been bombarded with, "But if we don't make them write a book report, they won't read!" and "How will we know if they've really read the book if we don't have them write a report?" I usually answer, "If they won't read unless you make them prove it, then your recreational reading program is a flop anyway." Furthermore, as McCracken and

McCracken (1978) point out, requiring proof that they have actually read the book only gives the students proof that you don't trust them. In addition, the proof usually required isn't proof at all. Any bright second grader can learn enough about a book from the first chapter or the book jacket to write a three-line summary of the book or to create a diorama about it, especially if the teacher has never read the book.

Occasionally, teachers will defend the practice by asserting that making an oral or written book report enhances the development of other skills, such as the ability to speak in front of a group or the ability to write a summary. However, the minute amount of sporadic practice that takes place when reporting about a book once a month can hardly justify coupling recreational reading with what may be a very odious task.

Many arguments can be put forth against requiring sharing after recreational reading. People read for many different purposes—for escape, to seek information, to experience something vicariously, to indulge curiosity, and so on. Demanding an accounting of any sort after recreational reading incurs the risk of subordinating the reader's very legitimate purposes to the teacher's purpose—accountability. Students learn to devalue their own purposes because these purposes are not reinforced. A few students may even get the idea that one doesn't read unless one is made accountable for it. As a result, some students may stop setting any purpose other than meeting the demands of accountability. In addition, the choice of reading material may also be altered to reflect the teacher's needs, not the child's. Shorter books and books that will be easy to be reported about may take the place of books the individual really wants to read. Under these conditions, some students not only will make little progress toward becoming independent, purposeful readers; they may actually regress.

Hunt (1970) emphasizes this point when he talks about "transcending the frustration level" (p. 147). He discusses readers who select books that are obviously too difficult for them to read with ease. But because the readers are highly motivated, they persevere. As Hunt points out, "Certainly in such instances the reader does not get all the ideas, not even all important ideas, but he does get enough to sustain his interest" (p. 148). To require that student to give a report on that book is to intrude the teacher's values upon what was for the *child* a very successful reading experience. Chances are the child will not have gained enough from the reading to meet the requirements for a report and, as a consequence, the feeling of success may be dimmed, if not quenched.

Requiring some sort of accountability after *every* free reading experience is especially suspect. One obvious drawback is that some children will actually be discouraged from reading as much as they like because they do not want to go through the onerous next step, the follow up. Therefore, they read less. This would be an unfortunate outcome for any recreational reading program.

In many classrooms a disagreeable adjunct to requiring book reports or other forced sharing is the nagging that comes about as the teacher tries to drag reports out of reluctant students. Surely such unpleasantness never instilled a love of reading in anyone.

Another reason for not requiring an accounting is that few classroom teachers need more records to keep or papers to peruse. The amount of paperwork needed to keep up with every book every child has read can be staggering.

McCracken and McCracken (1978), in discussing sustained silent reading, have come up with one simple test for the accountability issue:

> ... we suggest that teachers require nothing of children after sustained silent reading that they do not do themselves willingly and naturally. Usually this eliminates writing book reports, making lists of unknown words, filling in worksheets of any type, or taking tests. Sometimes this permits keeping a reading log or recording the title, author, and pages read. Usually this means talking about some of the ideas encountered, and sometimes recording the more important ideas for later use (p. 407).

I would like to urge two other tests. One, the sharing experience should be completely voluntary and optional, for both the person sharing and the listener. Two, during a recreational reading program the greatest amount of time should be spent in *reading,* not in recording books, giving reports, and completing related art projects.

Up to this point, all of the discussion has been focused on required sharing for the purpose of accountability. Voluntary sharing is a different matter and has much to recommend it. Many individuals enjoy sharing what they have read. They like discussing the ideas they've found and take pleasure in urging others to read something they have delighted in. These students should certainly be encouraged to share their reading experiences with willing listeners.

Voluntary sharing helps other students learn about new books and new kinds of books. Children who aren't quite sure what to read next or who want another book about crabgrass may find the selection process speeded up.

A last point for voluntary sharing is of particular concern for developing a love of reading. For those people who enjoy sharing (both as the one sharing and the one receiving), the sharing process can do much to reinforce enjoyment of reading. The individual comes to associate the pleasant camaraderie of sharing with reading itself and, therefore, the reader is likely to do even more reading. (Note how this effect is precisely opposite to that of requiring sharing. The key is the voluntary nature of the sharing.)

Guidelines for voluntary sharing. In this section you will *not* find 2,138 ways for children to share what they have read. What you will find are two guidelines for helping you select the best procedures for voluntary sharing from the myriad offered elsewhere. A few techniques will be given as examples of putting these guidelines into practice.

Guideline 1. The amount of time spent in preparing and presenting the sharing project should be much less than that spent in the original reading of the material shared. Too often a child will spend one hour reading a 28-page book and seven hours creating a clay model of the setting or preparing and presenting a three act musical review of the main events. Granted that the child did enjoy these artistic endeavors, somehow the proportions of time spent are all wrong for a recreational reading program.

Even voluntary book reports may take too much time. A quick alternative that some children may find attractive is the Six

Point Account (California Reading Association, 1977, p. 45).

1. Rename the story in 1 word.
2. Tell about the story in 2 words.
3. Name 3 people in the story.
4. Tell where most of the story took place in 4 words.
5. Give the names of people you know whom you would like to have read the story and tell why you would like to have them read it.
6. Illustrate a favorite part of the story.

(Personally, I think Step 6 could be omitted.)

Guideline 2. The sharing technique should be one that encourages or facilitates the recreational reading of others. The one exception to this is voluntarily sharing by discussing with the teacher what has been read. Techniques that involve the child in dealing with other students or in producing a tangible product should enhance the recreational reading of others in one of several ways. For example, the sharing technique could help others choose something to read. Criscuolo (1979) suggests that a class create a book catalog for their room reading center. A student finishing a book thought to be of interest to others could write a synposis of the book on 8" x 10" tagboard and perhaps draw a picture of an important event on the other side. The title, author, and location (school, classroom, or public library) could be written on the top. The catalog could be kept in a file box or held together by rings for easy access and easy expansion.

Eller and McClenathan (1978) point out that sharing does not have to be only about books the readers have liked. The children should also be encouraged to tell about books they did not like. Care should be taken, however, that the presenters are prepared to give specific reasons for disliking a book and not rely on a general "It just wasn't any good" type of comment. Sharing books that are not favorites not only guides others in their choices, it also helps develop critical consumers of written matter.

The sharing technique could also be used to provide reading pleasure for those who do not yet read well themselves. Both Indrisano (1978) and Cain (1978) suggest cross-classroom sharing of books read. A reader could prepare to read orally either a favorite part of an interesting book or an entire short book. Most children enjoy reading aloud, even if they are not particularly good readers themselves. Sharing a special book orally gives children a purpose for reading aloud and encourages careful preparation of the presentation. Poor readers who may be embarrassed by not being able to read on grade level can achieve status in this way by sharing one of their "easy" books with a younger class. And the young listeners learn that reading is fun.

Sharing what one has read can also be a form of sharing information of common interest and can spur another student toward further exploration of the topic. Students wishing to report on books about specific topics may invite those interested in those topics to come and listen to what they have found out. Ad hoc groups may be formed for the sole purpose of gathering and sharing information about a common topic. Unlike the information gathering groups described previously, these sharing groups would be formed only as individuals expressed a need. Only one or two such groups might be functioning at any one time.

Sharing what has been read can be stimulating and enjoyable, if the reader wants to share. Requiring sharing reduces reading to a task that one does because one has to, not because one wants to. In this section I have presented many ways of motivating the child to *want* to read. Hopefully, teachers will not need to resort to an accountability system with a rigid set of requirements.

INITIATING A RECREATIONAL
READING PROGRAM

An effective recreational reading program needs more to get started than a cheerful, "Today we are just going to read for a while." Careful preparation is required in several areas. The environment must be arranged so that it is conducive to free reading. The students must be prepared and will likely need to be guided through some of the initial procedures. Parents and adminstrators must be won over to the program.

Preparing the Environment

Many teachers have gone to considerable expense and have spent long hours creating an environment conducive to recreational reading. They have built reading lofts, lined old bathtubs with soft pillows, and brought in elaborate racks and other materials for displaying reading materials attractively. Undoubtedly, children enjoy these "extras" and are motivated to read by them. But the most important part of the environment of a recreational reading program is not material. It is the atmosphere in a room that invites children to read. It is an atmosphere of quiet, of unhurried pace, of "down time." In some classrooms this atmosphere may exist for substantial portions of the day. In other classrooms this atmosphere surrounds the students only during time specifically set aside for recreational reading. But the atmosphere must exist for at least part of the day if a recreational reading program is going to induce *all* children to read.

Many reports of ssr programs have quoted students as treasuring the ssr period because of the down time. For at least that part of the day or week a student can be in a completely quiet setting, relaxed, with no pressures or deadlines or worries about right answers. For both students and teachers, the tranquility is a pleasant change from the usual bustle and rush in many classrooms.

The teacher can do much to foster such an environment. If the recreational reading program includes an ssr period, the teacher can set rules that reinforce quiet and lack of movement. For instance, many proponents of ssr (e.g., McCracken, 1971) suggest that students must have everything they want to read at their desks when the ssr period begins. If a child is near the end of a book or suspects that book is going to begin to pall soon, the child should have a second choice immediately at hand. This rule eliminates the distracting movement of children getting up to select something else to read and it also does not allow "wigglers" to spend their ssr period wandering around the room.

Children will soon learn that the teacher means business. The first few days some children will be unprepared and either will not have selected anything at all or will read their selection in five minutes. In cases of no preparation, the teacher can provide something. Teachers report that students quickly learn that they would rather read something of their own choice than the teacher's choice. The teacher can provide something for those who finish early or just let them sit quietly. The rule is that, barring fire drills and tornado alerts, students are glued to their seats.

This same rule can be effective when recreational reading is part of the morning reading period. Children are required to have their reading materials at their desks when the reading period begins. Then, even though the students will be doing their recreational reading at different times during the period and there will be some movement as children change activities, at least movement will be reduced.

If a regular time is allotted for recreational reading, a "Do Not Disturb" sign might be placed at the door. This is not the time for teachers to visit or for the principal to draw the teacher aside for a conference. The teacher is supposed to be modeling silent reading. The principal's cooperation should also be enlisted in other ways. For example, no practice fire drills should be scheduled during this time.

Although elaborate arrangements need not be made for special places for reading, an abundance of comfortable reading sites with adequate lighting should be available. A few large pillows (get the PTA to donate some or haunt yard sales and thrift shops) might be handy. Children should be allowed to read in places other than their seats, *if* they make these choices before the beginning of the SSR period and *if* they can behave. (Most have no trouble with this.) During the regular school day students should be allowed to move out of their seats to more comfortable spots at will. But one move per reading period should be enough.

Many children can read in the midst of the most annoying distractions. These children have already created their own, internal reading environment and are of no concern here. (Getting them to *stop* reading and go to recess or do their math may be another matter.) A pleasant reading environment is crucial for students who are not "natural" readers, who are easily distracted, and who may be reluctant at first to just sit and read. For those children the environment itself may be the original enticement. Then, to their surprise, they usually discover that what they do in that environment (reading) isn't so bad after all.

Preparing the Students

If all students were enthusiastic readers, we wouldn't need planned recreational reading programs. Enthusiastic readers always manage to get their hands on books and pry some time out of their day for reading. Recreational reading programs are designed to *create* such enthusiasm. Therefore students have to be initiated carefully into such a program. Some will be reluctant, a few will be completely sure that this is really dumb, and others will be willing to try it only because it's better than doing workbook pages.

The first step is to share with the children the purposes of a recreational reading program. Teachers should tell their classes what their goals are for the program and should invite the students to react to these goals. Classes should also feel free to add goals of their own or to set personal goals. Perhaps a class goal chart might be created and posted, with the teacher's goals for the group forming the central portion of the chart, surrounded by the satellite goals of individual students. This chart could be reviewed periodically as teacher and class assess the progress of the program. In addition, as children alter their own goals they could be encouraged to update their portion of the chart.

Class Goals Chart

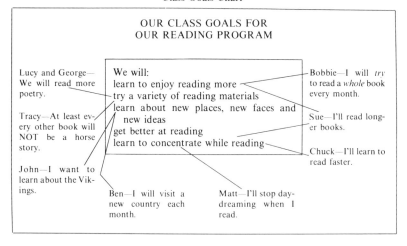

The students should feel as much as possible that this is their recreational reading program. Cooperatively setting goals will aid in this. Drawing up a set of rules for the program and giving students responsibility for enforcing these rules will personalize the program. Naturally, teachers will have some rules they feel must be included. Some of these may have been discussed earlier, such as restricting movement and permitting no

Practice

interruptions. Teachers should have little difficulty in getting the class to accept these suggested rules if they arise naturally out of class and personal goal statements. If these rules don't spring forth spontaneously, then teachers would be wise to reconsider the wisdom of the rules and/or the completeness of the goals.

Hopefully, the students' inspection of the goals will lead them to come up with the teacher's intended rules, among others. If not, a little "guiding" may be necessary. The complete set of rules should be posted and, as with the goal statements, should be reviewed often. As the program begins to function smoothly and automatically, the class may agree that some of the rules may be deleted. On the other hand, as faulty aspects of the program become apparent, the students may suggest other rules to eliminate these problems.

The next step is to begin the recreational reading itself. This should be done gradually and may start with the teacher reading aloud to the class for 10 minutes or so, followed by the class doing their personal reading for a short period of time. Slowly the proportions of time given to listening and individual reading should be reversed, so that most of the time is spent by the children reading. (But never give up reading to your class.) Some children may wish to do their own reading right from the beginning and they should be given that choice. Others, however, may need to experience the pleasure of hearing someone else read, closely followed by their own reading, before they are convinced that reading might actually be fun.

Most proponents of SSR suggest that the amount of time allotted to uninterrupted reading be very short at first. This advice is also sound if students are expected to do personal reading during the reading period. Some authors have given suggested time frames, such as 5-10 minutes for first or second graders and 15-20 minutes for intermediate students. However, classes vary in their ability to sustain such an activity and teachers would be wise to use their own knowledge about their classes as the starting point. McCracken (1971) suggests an individualized way of deciding how long the period should be. He recommends that the teacher decide upon a conservative amount of time to be spent and set a timer. (I would suggest a nonticking variety.) The amount of time chosen should not be announced to the class or some students will turn into clock watchers. When the timer rings, the teacher should announce that the class has read for X minutes and they may keep on reading if they like. Then the teacher should note when the first child quits reading and should use *that* time, minus a minute or two, as the allotment for the next period. For example, if the timer is set for 5 minutes and the first student to stop reading quits at 7 minutes, 6 minutes might be a good estimate for the next day. In this way, class reading time is gradually lengthened, but only in response to the students' observed ability to sustain reading for that long.

This technique of allowing the children to continue *after* the timer has rung can help to avoid clock watching. Of course some children will always be waiting anxiously for the time to end. But if the timer is used only to indicate the beginning of the second phase (i.e., reading from then until you're tired of it), clock watchers may be less concerned with the number of minutes that have passed.

Gambrell (1978) warns that any recreational reading program needs variety to keep it going. SSR may be a valuable starting point because it is very structured. In addition, SSR and the attendant rules will help students become more aware of the kind of environment needed for personal reading. Furthermore, many students will become convinced of the joy of reading simply because, through SSR, they have had to do it for the first time. But after these points have been won, variations might be introduced to keep the program from becoming stale. Some of these variations have been described previously under "Grouping Procedures." Other variations can come about through motivational techniques and sharing procedures.

Another reason for introducing variety into the recreational reading program is the problem of transfer. We don't want children to read *only* during prescribed times. Therefore the more ways in which we can give them opportunities to read, the more likely, they are to find their own opportunities.

One final word of caution: Don't give up quickly. Many children (and adults) have learned that if they resist even for a little while, they can win. The idea of sitting down and sticking to a book for 5 or 10 minutes is new to many students and they need to practice before they can do it successfully. Don't give up if they haven't been won over in the first week; hang in there for at least a month. You'll find it's really worth it.

Preparing Parents

The students need some preparation for "just" reading. Teachers need to convince themselves that a recreational reading program is worth the time and effort. Similarly, parents must be convinced of the value of such a program. Some parents may feel that teachers who aren't actually instructing are not earning their salaries. Others may see a recreational reading program as a frill and may key in on the word *recreational* as meaning outside of the basic curriculum.

Making the Initial Contact

Before actually beginning the program, the cooperation of parents should be enlisted in two ways: 1) a letter or other form of communication should explain to parents how the program will work and what the rationale for the program is, and 2) the parents' help should be solicited.

The initial presentation of the program is very important and can be made in several ways. One way is to communicate to the parents through some sort of a newsletter. I would suggest spreading the presentation across several letters rather than overwhelming parents by both content and quantity of ideas in one letter. Most of us don't like reading long mimeographed letters from anyone, so if the ideas are presented in several newsletters, spaced across a week or so, chances are more parents will actually read the information.

Other reasons for spacing out the information are the novelty of a recreational reading program and some individual's instinctual initial resistance to anything new. The teacher should give out the new ideas in little doses, giving each dose time to "take" before dispensing another. However, parents must be aware that more information is coming and when, or else the teacher will be deluged with phone calls after the first epistle goes home. Perhaps a schedule like this would be appropriate:

Newletter 1. Explanation of what a recreational reading program is and how it will work in your class. Schedule of what information will be contained in subsequent newsletters.

Newsletter 2 (two days later). Rationale for having a recreational reading program, with emphasis on how it fits into the basic curriculum. Short statement of support from your principal and reading teacher.

Newsletter 3 (two days later). List of suggestions of ways parents can help support the program through their efforts at home.

Newsletter 4 (two days later). List of ways parents can volunteer their time in the classroom to support this program.

Another way to initiate parents into the recreational reading program is through personal contact during School Visitation Night. An invitation could be sent asking each parent who plans to attend to bring something they want to read "just for fun." (The teacher should have a variety of materials available in the classroom for parents who forget to bring something to read.) Then the first 5 minutes of the classroom visit could be spent in SSR. Many parents will enjoy the pleasant, non-threatening atmosphere of SSR, just as their children will, and will then be more likely to listen to the explanation of the program in a more positive frame of mind.

A combination of the newsletters and the personal touch is probably wise, since many parents are unable or unwilling to attend school open houses. Parents have the right to know what is going on in their schools. If the teacher takes the initiative in presenting this information, parents will get the message that a recreational reading program is something the teacher really believes in and is proud of.

Suggestions for Support at Home

Few teachers would dispute the importance of the home environment to creating enthusiastic and able readers. Research supports this notion. For example, Ryan (1977) found that college freshmen in remedial English did not read as well as their counterparts in regular English courses. Furthermore, a questionnaire elicited the following information from remedial students as a group:

> they were read to less often as children, they have a fewer number and a smaller variety of books in the home, their parents read less and had more difficulty with reading in school, there is less interest in and evidence of reading in their homes, and their immediate relatives have been less-successful readers (p. 162).

L. Wells et al. (cited in R. Wells, 1978) studied fifth grade students and found two qualities about parents that induced children to read: "supportiveness (providing interesting reading material) and arousal of interest" (p. 22). They also identified three negative parental factors: "overstress on reading, punishment, and parent-induced frustration" (p. 22). Sauls (1971) found a significant relationship between the number of books read by sixth grade students and the amount of home encouragement for reading. Not only do parents have an important effect on their children's reading habits, but most parents genuinely do want to help, especially when basic skills are the issue. All experienced teachers have met parents who have planned a home program involving 1-2 hours a night of practice and instruction. Such parents are well motivated, but most teachers would agree that such an intensive program would do more harm than good. Enlisting parental support for a recreational reading program provides parents with something specific to do to assist their child's school progress, but limits these activities to low-pressure, pleasurable interactions.

One of the most important things parents can do to support a recreational reading program is to create what Cain (1978) calls a "reading culture." By this she means that parents and teachers should "immerse children in the thriving climate of literacy that leads to reading" (p. 64). Parents can do this at home simply by being models, by letting their children see them reading and using reading in their everyday activities. Many families have learned to enjoy a home SSR period during which *everyone* in the family sits down together and reads something of their choice. The adults may be reading newspapers or magazines or cookbooks. The children may page through picture books or children's magazines or read from books. Parents should *not* be doing their own "homework" at this time, i.e., things brought home from the office. This family SSR time should be truly recreational reading.

Of course, reading aloud to children is something many parents treasure and do as often as possible. Other parents may feel that children do not get to practice their own reading if parents do the reading. Some parents may also feel that at certain ages children may be too old to be read to. Teachers need to convince these parents that reading to someone and being read to helps reinforce the pleasure of reading for both the reader and the listener, regardless of age. For parents who are still unconvinced, the buddy system might be suggested: children read to the parents until they tire, and then the parents read for a spell.

Teachers can further encourage reading at home by providing parents with annotated suggestions of good books to read to their children or for children to read themselves. These suggestions could be incorporated into the weekly newsletter, along with guidelines for matching child and book. For example, a particular book might be touted as of special value for the Redbird reading group to read.

Often parents will be unsure of the difficulty of a book they find on their own and an Easy Reading label is sometimes deceptive. Teachers can urge parents to let a child "try out" a book, with the understanding that the youngster should be perfectly free to say, "This is a book I want *you* to read to *me*," or "I don't want to read this book."

Teachers should mount a real crusade to get parents to obtain public library cards for themselves and their children. Some library systems will permit teachers to collect applications for cards. Teachers can also make parents aware of library locations and hours and of bookmobile schedules. Maps showing the location of the public library in relation to grocery stores and other shopping areas may be useful. Announcements of special services available at the library and of special events should be routine parts of the class newletter. Some parents may even be interested in weekly car pooling for transporting children to and from the library on a regular basis. Teachers can assist in making the initial contacts. Many adults are not in the habit of using libraries at all and teachers need to make parents aware of how valuable and inexpensive the public library is.

Many parents wish they could do more to help out in the classroom but because of working outside the home or pressures at home these individuals cannot volunteer. The recreational reading program offers these parents opportunities to be of real value to the school while still meeting their other commitments. Perhaps the most important way in which they can help is in the gathering of reading materials for the classroom library. Teachers can ask parents to send their children's castoff books to school. Old issues of children's magazines, *National Geographic,* and *Reader's Digest* can be solicited. Some parents may be willing to ask their neighbors to look through their attics and basements for unwanted books. Others may suggest that church groups or service organizations become involved in collecting reading material. These groups could even "adopt" particular classrooms and thus provide their adopted children with new books as well as used ones. They even may be willing to sponsor a subscription to a children's magazine such as *Ranger Rick* for the class. Interested parents can spark the initial involvement of such groups and then let the groups themselves sustain the effort.

Suggestions for Support at School

Some parents are both willing and able to come into the classroom on a volunteer basis and a recreational reading program can make use of such volunteers in many ways. Teachers should send a list of these ways to the parents, along with a sincere welcome. This will not only make the willing volunteers feel needed; it may also encourage others who want to help but don't feel capable of offering instructional assistance.

If a classroom has an SSR period, volunteers can come and serve as adult models for silent reading. This role as a model would be a particularly appropriate first job for a new volunteer who lacks confidence. McEachern (1980) found that using SSR with adults improved their own attitudes about reading, so this modeling could have some important side benefits.

After SSR, some volunteers may also be willing to serve as models for sharing what they have read. Others may be listeners as children seek to share with just one person rather than with the whole class. The use of parent volunteers as listeners affords the children in the classroom additional opportunities to share reading with an adult. One teacher can listen to only a few children each day.

Parents can volunteer to read to children—to whole classrooms, to small groups, or to individuals. The books read could be the students' choice or could be something the volunteer wishes to share. Some parents may even be willing to prepare and present Book Talks.*

A recreational reading program can survive without parent volunteers in the classroom but such adult assistance can make the difference between surviving and flourishing. I'm not sure the program can even survive without support at home. The students may seem to be eager to participate while at school, but one wonders if they will transfer this enthusiasm to their lives outside the classroom without parental encouragement. The teacher who does not seek parental support for a recreational reading program is taking a big risk.

Preparing the Administration

Teachers who do not seek the support of the principal may be running an even larger risk than teachers who bypass parental support. Principals need to know what is going on in their buildings. After all, they may be the ones who receive querying phone calls about a certain teacher's recreational reading program. No principal wants to have to admit to not knowing what's going on in any teacher's program.

A teacher planning to initiate a recreational reading program should talk with the principal before even mentioning the program to children or parents. This does not mean that the teacher can go to the principal with a fuzzy idea of what the

---

*Teachers interested in articles on parent involvement should consult N.L. Quisenberry, C. Blakemore, and C.A. Warren. Involving parents: An annotated bibliography. *Reading Teacher*, 1977, *31*(1), 34-39.

program should be—the teacher should have a thorough presentation for the principal. This presentation should describe the program briefly and give a complete rationale with special emphasis on how the program fits into the regular curriculum and how time will be found for the program.

Next, the teacher should outline what needs the program will have, such as a modest paperback budget, parent volunteers, free access to the library, and changes in schedules. A wise teacher will keep initial requests at a minimum so that the principal will not need to make major concessions of either time or money. Beginning with a single classroom program with existing supplies may be the best first step. Then after the success of the initial, limited program the teacher can begin "maneuvering" for expansion.

At the time of the initial request, the teacher may also share ways in which the principal can give moral support to the program. I have already mentioned a statement of support to parents in the classroom newsletter. The principal might also visit the classroom occasionally to serve as a reading model if an SSR period is used and might try to find time regularly to talk with children about what they have read (see Book Look Lunches, mentioned previously). Such personal participation in the program will help to convince the principal that the recreational reading program is valuable and is serving an important purpose in the curriculum.

A good recreational reading program will run smoothly with very little effort *once* it is off the ground. The initial preparation of environment, students, parents, and administration, however, takes very careful planning. It is in this initial phase that many recreational reading programs whimper to a stop, but this failure is needless and is easily avoided with a little cautious preparation.

MANAGING TIME FOR RECREATIONAL READING

Most daily schedules for elementary and intermediate grade classrooms are already bulging with "musts." The teacher must teach reading, writing, and arithmetic. And social studies, science, spelling, and health. And maybe art, music, and physical education. And then there are children going to the reading teacher, the speech therapist, the LD resource teacher, band practice, programs for the gifted and talented, and so on. In spite of the resulting 3-ring circus atmosphere, most teachers would be able to find time for one 30-minute period of SSR a week.

In this section, however, I would like to explore finding *other* opportunities for recreational reading. One goal of a recreational reading program is to develop in children the *habit* of choosing to read. Habits are not likely to be developed if they are practiced only once a week and then only at a specific signal. Teachers should try to saturate their daily schedules with opportunities during which children may choose to read or not. To do this, teachers need to look for opportunities to slip in reading during the regular schedule and for ways to revise their schedules to provide more free-reading time.

Slipping Recreational Reading into the Schedule

By slipping opportunities to read into the daily schedule, a teacher can lead children toward the realization that it is very natural to use any free moment to pick up a book and read. Children should begin to understand that books and reading belong everywhere. To reinforce this idea, teachers should have a book at hand almost all of the time. They should let the students see that adults tend to pick up a book during brief idle moments—when waiting for lunch or while supervising a bathroom break. Of course, I am not suggesting that you keep your nose in a book while your charges run wild through the halls. That would guarantee a very short career. But if your students can tolerate less than complete supervision, divide your activities between reading and supervising.

The children must learn to recognize and seize spontaneous opportunities for reading and plan accordingly. If one wants to be able to seize an opportunity one has to follow the Boy Scout motto: Be prepared. Have a book with you.

Teachers can encourage preparedness by requiring students to have a piece of recreational reading matter at their desks at all times. Bus riders can be strongly urged to take a book along, even though the cacaphony may distract all but the most dedicated. (Actually, if enough teachers did this and the bus drivers knew that the children had something to read, life might be a lot more pleasant on a school bus.) When waiting in an assembly for the rest of the classes to file in, the children can read, courteously placing their books under their chairs when the program is about to begin. Teachers can have spot checks on who has a book at the ready, rewarding those who do with lavish praise or other honors (but *not* punishing those without).

Often during the day students need a "settling down" period. For students who change classrooms this time may come at the very beginning or at the end of the class. After lunch or recess or after a particularly invigorating discussion, many children need an abrupt change of pace in order to simmer down. A short spell of ssr can accomplish this, especially if the children's reading matter is always right at hand. The key to seizing opportunities to slip in reading at any point is having something to read at that moment.

Revising Existing Practices and Schedules

Go get your lesson plan book right now and two different colored pencils. (Use pens if you're a very decisive person!) Now, in one color go through last week's plans and mark every time period in which you might have either combined recreational reading with another activity or deleted a teacher-directed activity and replaced it with free reading. Next, take the other colored pencil and mark every time you could have replaced a specified independent activity with free reading without any real loss of learning.

I hope you were able to find some time, even five minutes, each day for recreational reading with only minor changes in your plans. Let's compare notes.

Were you willing to give up your basal lesson once a week to give your students practice time? You could devote all of Friday's one to one-and-one-half hour reading period to recreational reading. Better yet would be to have one reading group a day involved with free reading rather than meeting with the teacher in the basal group. With this plan, the teacher can use that extra half hour or so for extended work with other groups or with individuals. Furthermore, the students are not compelled to read for an entire hour (which is a long time for many youngsters).

Did you find a way to change your plans to implement Smith and Johnson's three-group plan (described previously)? Did you take a long look at your social studies and science plans for ways to incorporate free (or semi-free) reading into the lessons. For example, if the class is studying electricity or South America or mammals, a temporary minilibrary might be available on that topic. The teacher could collect magazine articles, biographies, works of fiction, and supplementary science or social studies texts. For the last 10 minutes or so of the period, the students could be allowed to read something related to the topic. This, of course, is not completely free recreational reading, but it does allow children to find time to read something other than a standard text and to select from several choices. In addition, this procedure can introduce children to information-gathering through reading and may expand their reading interests beyond routine fiction. As a class, their knowledge of the topic under study will be enhanced as students share additional information from their individual reading.

Perhaps the easiest way to find time for recreational reading is to alter the independent activities required of the students. Unfortunately, many teachers feel compelled to take every child through every page in a workbook and every activity suggested in a manual. (As one teacher replied when I challenged this practice, "We paid for these workbooks so we're going to do every page!") As a result, children often spend valuable free reading time doing workbook or ditto pages that they really don't need to do. Teachers should cast a critical eye at every page *before* assigning it. If the teacher feels confident that a particular child does need to practice the skill on that page, then the student should be assigned that page. Conversely, some children will already have mastered that skill, and to have them complete that page insults them and wastes their time. Let them practice *using* the skill in recreational reading.

If the teacher is not sure whether certain children may have learned that skill, there is a relatively easy solution. The children should be required to do half of the items on the page, such as all the even items or the first half. If the children score 100 percent on those items, then most likely they do not need to do the rest of the page. This procedure has several advantages: Students do not waste time doing something already mastered; students now can use that time for recreational reading; students are motivated to do their best, thereby avoiding the rest of the work. And the teacher only has to grade half the amount of work. (That leaves the *teacher* some time for recreational reading at home—a true rarity!)

In addition to questioning the appropriateness of specific workbook and ditto pages, teachers need to examine other routine practices. Perhaps the students don't need to write their spelling words in sentences *every* week. Can a penmanship lesson be combined with a language arts lesson and the resulting free time be used for reading? Teachers need to look creatively at their weekly plans instead of automatically putting down what they have "always" done. The world will not end if spelling is ignored once every two weeks in favor of recreational reading.

Now go back to your plans for this week or next week. For every day find a minimum of 10 minutes for recreational reading. Be daring. Take a risk and just cross out something routine. If it's a mistake, you and the children will survive. But try many different ways to put recreational reading into each day. Through this experimentation you will find what works best for you and your students.

Transferring Recreational Reading to the Home Front

Earlier, I described ways in which parents can encourage recreational reading at home. Teachers can assist this process in two additional ways. First, they can follow the rule of preparedness and make sure that each child has something to read at home, especially for the weekend. This may entail a check shortly after lunch and some quick trips by individuals to the school library. It most certainly will involve a fairly substantial and *freely circulating* classroom library. It may involve a certain amount of nagging until the children realize that it's going to be hard to make it out of the room at three o'clock without something to read.

The second way in which teachers can help transfer recreational reading from the school to the home is to reward reading at home, as well as at school. Many children are so involved with other activities at home that they just don't have or take the time to read. This lack of time, in the face of demands of "homework, religious activities, sports events, and social organizations" (Heathington, 1979, p. 710), is a real problem. Long and Henderson (1973) found that reading ranked only above "chores" in amount of time spent outside school. The fifth graders in Long and Henderson's study reported spending an average of 30.3 hours in two weeks watching television, 20.0 hours in free play, 8.3 hours in organized play, 7.7 hours doing homework, 3.1 hours reading, and 2.4 hours doing chores. If these figures are typical, teachers need to do a lot of public relations work in order to convince their students that reading is a reasonable alternative to other activities.

Finding time for recreational reading will be more difficult in some classes than in others. Some teachers may need to make major revisions in their daily schedules. Others may find it easy to slip recreational reading into their day. In either case, conscious plans must be made in order to ensure that children do have several opportunities each day to read something of their own choosing.

MANAGING MATERIALS FOR A
RECREATIONAL READING PROGRAM

For a recreational reading program to be a success the participants must have a large variety of easily accessible reading materials. These materials must be available in the classroom, in the school library, and at home.

Maintaining a Classroom Library

The importance of a large, freely-circulating classroom library cannot be overestimated, both for in-class recreational reading and voluntary reading outside of the classroom. Bissett (1969) found that students who had in their classroom a large paperback library (259 books) read an average of 11.76 books in 15 weeks, whereas those students with "regular" classroom libraries and procedures only reported reading an average of 8.56 books. When the large library was combined with 90 minutes a week of adults and students talking about books they had read, the number of books read jumped to an average of 22.67.

Lamme (1976) followed the reading habits of one group of children as they progressed from fourth through sixth grade. She found that the children's most important sources of reading matter were the classroom and school libraries. Other sources were rarely used. Lamme further concluded that classroom libraries were important only if teachers encouraged their use and if the contents of these libraries were changed from time to time.

Sources of Materials

As Bissett and Lamme's research has shown, a classroom library has to be stocked with a large number of books and these books have to change periodically. Tired, dusty collections of 10-year-old books will do little to entice reluctant readers to read and voracious readers will make short work of such limited collections. However, few teachers have the wealth to personally stock their classroom libraries and many school budgets are too limited to provide much assistance. Therefore, most teachers will have to look to other sources for funds for books and for books themselves.

In the section on parents (described previously in this booklet), several suggestions were given for ways parents can help build classroom libraries. Teachers should not neglect garage sales and thrift shops as sources to get the most for their own money. In addition, secondhand bookstores often have substantial bargains, especially on paperbacks.

Outdated textbooks can be rich resources for the classroom library. Gambrell (1978) suggests cutting old basals apart and making individual booklets out of the separate stories. These minibooks can be very attractive to poor readers who are intimidated by the amount of reading in an entire book. Teachers must be sure, however, that these minibooks have the status of regular books and are not perceived as "baby" books by the children or by the teachers.

Entire texts may be valuable, too, especially for nonfiction reading at an appropriate grade level. Often it is difficult to find science and social studies reading matter at low readability levels. Even slightly out-of-date science books can provide enjoyable reading, especially for the beginner.

Many commercial book clubs can provide teachers and children with relatively inexpensive paperback selections. For teachers, the great advantage of many of these clubs is the bonus system, whereby teachers can order a free book for every X books the students order. Volunteer groups (such as parent-teacher organizations or church groups) who wish to donate new books to classroom libraries might get the most for their money by ordering through the classroom's book club.

Teachers may arrange trades with other teachers so that the composition of an individual classroom library changes every two months or so. For example, Teacher A and Teacher B, who both teach third grade, may each select 25 books from their libraries to loan to the other for two months. Another time, Teacher A may trade with Teacher C, who teaches a different grade level. Traders would be wise to keep in mind that a selection of "winners" will help ensure that they don't get only "losers" in return. The traded collection should be well-balanced and attractive.

A large classroom library is indispensible to a recreational reading program, but teachers do not need to spend large amounts of their own money to stock it. A little hustle to solicit donations from volunteer groups and a little thrifty comparison shopping can keep most classroom libraries in thriving condition.

Selecting Materials

Since the students are the ones who are going to be doing the reading, perhaps the students should have a large voice in the selection of the reading matter for the classroom library. They may earn the right to be on the committee to select books or this right may simply rotate among all the class members.

However the ordering is done, a good classroom library must have a wide variety of reading matter, covering a broad range of readabilities. Teachers must be wary of choosing materials that meet their own preconceived notions of what their students like or what they *should* be reading. Perhaps the safest route is to stick with variety, selecting from many topics and difficulty levels.

Picture books. All sorts of reading matter have value. For example, Watson (1978) recommends that picture books not be limited to the primary grades but be included in libraries for middle grade students as well. He makes this suggestion not for the value of picture books to the poor reader (which, of course, they do have) but for their utility in developing higher level comprehension, such as the understanding of satire.*

---

*Watson includes a bibliography of suggested picture books in his article.

Television tie-ins. Although some teachers may want to concentrate on "good" literature, the students may have other ideas. Books related to television shows have proved to be very popular with young people. McKenzie (cited in Coil, 1978) discovered that 36 of the 50 most popular books read by junior and senior high school students had TV or movie tie-ins. Hamilton (1976) found that junior high students chose books with TV tie-ins in a ratio of 23:10 over books without a relationship to TV. Tie-ins were of particular interest to students with a low socioeconomic background and with low IQs. In addition, boys appeared to be more influenced by the television tie-ins than did girls.

Comic books. Comic books are another kind of reading material sometimes scorned by teachers. Negin (1978), however, points out that comic books have many favorable characteristics. They may broaden interests; their vivid images are a boon to readers without a great deal of imagination; students are interested in the contemporary settings of many comics and identify with their use of common speech patterns; the abundance of action motivates many reluctant readers to try reading; comics are inexpensive; children find it easy to identify with the familiar characters in comics; and comics are representative of American folklore.

Ample evidence exists to show that young readers do enjoy comic books. Brown, Engin, and Wallbrown (1979) found that innercity students in the intermediate grades did read comics and that this tendency increased slightly from fourth to sixth grades. Greaney and Quinn (1978) noted that boys spent more time with comic books that did girls.

On the other hand, all the news about comics and reading is not good. Arlin and Roth (1978) observed third graders who had both comic books and books available for free reading. They found that students spent about the same amount of time looking at comics as at books. Thus, concludes Guthrie (1978), comics have no better and no worse potential for sustaining attention. However, observations of time actually spent in reading these materials indicated that poor readers only read comics for an average of 5 minutes, whereas they read books for an average of 12 minutes. In other words, most of their time was used in looking at pictures. For good readers there were no real differences between behavior with comics and books. Although poor readers may spend as much time with comics as with books, they may not derive as many benefits from their reading. Nevertheless, teachers should consider including some comics in their libraries to lure less motivated students into at least some form of reading.

Paperback books. Most of the discussion so far about stocking classroom libraries has assumed that paperback books will form a large part of any library. Some individuals may resist paperbacks because they are easily mangled and therefore need to be replaced often. The advantages of paperbacks, however, far outweigh their disadvantages. With the cost of hardbound books soaring, a teacher can buy several paperback copies for the price of one clothbound book. In addition, paperbacks are small and easily stored in a desk or locker, so that they are *available* to be read. No one is going to lug a three-pound book around when the same book is available in a three-ounce version.

A study by Lowery and Grafft done several years ago (1965) showed that the use of paperback books significantly increased attitudes toward reading. Students with the same titles available in clothbound versions had no change in attitude. Lowery and Grafft suggest that many students may associate clothbound books with failure in school since most texts have hard covers. Furthermore, they hypothesized that the small size and ease of handling of paperbacks may encourage a feeling of possession or ownership.

If individuals wish to donate new books to the classroom library and seem more interested in clothbound books than in paperbacks, teachers might recommend Caldecott award books (books recognized for their superior illustrations). The wonderful graphics in these books are sometimes diminished by the reduction to paperback size and printing methods and, therefore, these books are often better purchased in hardcover. In addition, many books are not available in paperback. Teachers should keep a list of these handy for persons seeking recommendations for special donations.

Lists of recommended books. Over the years, many lists of books for specific groups of children or on particular topics or genres have been developed. Teachers wishing to consult such lists need only ask their school or public librarian to direct them to these sources. Here I am only going to describe four lists and one additional ongoing source of recommendations.

Lance Gentile and Merna McMillan. Humor and the reading program. *Journal of Reading*, 1978, *21*(4), 343-349. The authors have developed a partial bibliography of trade materials, comics, and cartoons for the different stages of humor for ages 10-16 and above. (The stages of humor are based on A. Gessell, F.L. Ilg, and L.B. Ames. *Youth: The years from ten to sixteen.* New York: Harper and Row, 1956, 343-346.)

Alden Moe and Carol Hopkins. Jingles, jokes, limericks, poems, proverbs, puns, puzzles, and riddles: Fast reading for reluctant readers. *Language Arts*, 1978, *55*(8), 957-965; 1003. This annotated bibliography describes short, quickly read materials and indicates if the materials would be of interest to primary, intermediate, or junior high students.

Michael F. Graves, Judith A. Boettcher, and Randall J. Ryder. *Easy Reading.* Newark, Delaware: International Reading Association, 1979. Available through IRA, this booklet includes annotations on book series and periodicals for less able readers.

Jo Stanchfield and S.R. Fraim. A follow-up study on the reading interests of boys. *Journal of Reading*, 1979, *22*(8), 748-752. The authors list books and magazines that junior high boys found enjoyable.

For five years, IRA and the Children's Book Council have conducted "try-outs" of new children's books throughout the United States and have compiled an annual annotated bibliography that includes children's reactions to the books. The books are grouped under various genre and age level headings. Reprints of the yearly bibliography are free and may be obtained from:

Children's Choices
The Children's Book Council

67 Irving Place
New York, N.Y. 10003

A self-addressed envelope, stamped to accommodate 2 oz., should be included.

Because real children do not fit into neat, premolded categories, teachers should be wary of looking only to outside sources for advice in selecting material for a classroom library. Two guidelines should be kept in mind: 1) strive for variety and 2) let the children themselves participate in the selection process.

Keeping a Classroom Library Circulating

Once a sufficient quantity of desirable reading matter has been acquired, the teacher must find ways to arrange these materials so that students can easily find what they want. The teacher must also decide on circulation policies that enhance, not hinder use of the classroom library.

Arranging the library. Probably the most important aspect of arranging a classroom library is visibility. If books are hidden away in boxes or in hard-to-get-at shelves, they will not be read. Sometimes books are piled on tables with the idea that they will be readily available. However, if too many books are on the table, selection is hampered because there is no systematic way to browse. With shelves, a large number of books can be investigated in a systematic manner. Only space equivalent to the spine's width is needed, whereas with table displays one must accommodate a much larger surface.

If shelf space is limited, books may be displayed on a rotating basis. Every month part of the library can be temporarily retired and replaced with books that have been out of circulation for the past month. Hopefully, the retired books can be stored in a place where the students *can* peruse them if they are willing to look through a box of books.

Many teachers do not make any attempt to organize their classroom libraries. They feel that any scheme for arranging the books on the shelves will only be in operation fleetingly, since the children are not particularly concerned with reshelving books in any order. Furthermore, these teachers have found that a lack of systematic arrangement does not keep their students from finding books they want.

Other teachers are more comfortable with a loose system for shelving reading material in some order. One system that might work is a dot technique. Colored press-on plastic dots are put on books spines to indicate their category. For example, one yellow dot might mean a sports story, two red dots would be used for animal stories, and one red and one yellow dot would signal a book about other lands. All the yellow-dotted books would be shelved together so that a student interested in sports stories could easily find a book of that kind.

If a card catalog were available for the classroom library or if extensive sharing of books were done by the students (thus alerting others to certain books by specific authors), a rough alphabetizing system might be used within categories. In other words, all books by authors whose names begin with A would precede all books by authors whose names begin with B. But within the As, no attempt would be made to alphabetize.

Keeping books arranged by topic and/or author may not be as impossible as some suggest. If the students find the categorization or alphabetization useful, they will most likely volunteer occasionally to straighten up the library. Most classrooms have one or two budding librarians who enjoy keeping the books in order. In the lower grades the teacher can even assign the alphabetizing task on the basis of need to practice alphabetizing.

The one person who should *not* be greatly involved in keeping the books in order is the teacher. It's the children's library. If they feel a need for maintaining a category or alphabetical system, they will maintain it. If the students don't find these systems useful, then the teacher shouldn't squander precious time arranging the books.

One last minor point about arranging the classroom library deserves mention. If at all possible, the library should be placed in an area that encourages browsing. Of course, many classrooms are so crowded with children and furniture that the teacher feels fortunate to find a place for the library itself. But if choices exist, the library should be in a physically inviting area with some open space to flop down and try out a book for a few minutes. Especially undesirable are shelves placed immediately behind students' desks or the teacher's desk, so that anyone looking for a book is likely to disturb the person at the desk. Teachers with movable furniture should consider these factors when arranging their rooms. Teachers with fixed furniture may find their options are also fixed and will just have to do the best they can.

Circulation policies. As far as a classroom library is concerned, circulation policies should exist for the sole purpose of facilitating circulation. Any policy that limits circulation should be immediately discarded.

This means that books will get lost occasionally and the teacher will not be able to track down the culprits. So what? To me it doesn't seem worth the time and effort to keep track of all books in order to be able to replace the several dollars' worth of books lost each year. Furthermore, the unpleasantness of punishing an eight-year-old will do nothing to encourage recreational reading.

Two potential circulation problems may require some attention. One problem is the child who will select a book and then keep it forever, thus effectively removing that book from circulation. Having a two-week limit on any book is not an effective solution. In the first place, such a time limit means someone has to keep track of when books are taken out and also has to badger the students to return overdue books. In addition, a set time limit does not take into account the nature of the book, the size of the book, the purpose for which it was selected, or the reading speed of the student who chose it. A better solution is an honor system whereby students follow a simple rule of thumb: If you haven't read at least X more pages in the book or spent X minutes reading it this week, return it. The amount of reading required could vary according to the student and, in any case, should be a very conservative figure. In this way, one circulation bottleneck can be at least minimized if not avoided, and with a limited amount of hassle and record-keeping.

A second circulation problem that may necessitate teacher intervention is that of very popular books. Two simple solutions are available: Waiting lists and multiple copies. In the case of waiting lists, time limits unfortunately may need to be imposed on the readers, although varied time limits for individuals would still be best. Multiple copies of favorite books can help avoid the whole problem. With so many popular books available in paperback editions, teachers would be wise to buy several copies of favorites even if this practice means purchasing a smaller variety of reading materials.

Insofar as circulation is concerned, the only reason I can think of for having children sign out books is to find out which books are most popular. This information can be useful when ordering material for the classroom library. It can also help the teacher with a rotating library decide which books are of least interest to this particular group of students and, therefore, are the best candidates for temporary retirement.

The easiest way to get this information is to attach gummed Date Due slips to the books. As children read a book, they sign and date the slip. Then periodically the teacher (or an interested student) can go through the library and note which books have languished on the shelf and which have been read by several students.

The classroom library is the core of any recreational reading program. But the library must be stocked with a large variety of reading material truly of interest to the students. The library must be arranged so that children can easily find books they want. Circulation policies should be designed to keep books circulating and not for financial accountability. A recreational reading program simply cannot function with limited circulation of a few dull books.

Enlisting the Cooperation of the School Librarian

Some schools call them Instructional Materials Center (IMC) directors or coordinators. Some call them librarians. Regardless of what they are called, the individuals in charge of school libraries or instructional materials centers can be priceless allies in the development and maintenance of recreational reading programs. These professionals can be of assistance in two major ways. First, they can use procedures within their own domain—the library—that encourage easy access to reading materials. Second, they can become part of the school's motivational program to get children excited about reading.

Library Procedures to Enhance Recreational Reading

Obviously, the most important way a librarian can cooperate with a recreational reading program is to ensure that a student will always have something at hand to read. Practices that limit a child to one book per visit run counter to this effort. Of course, if the school library is very small, children may need to be restricted to two or three books. But just one book is deadly. Children may find they do not like a particular book after all, or that it's too hard, or that they have already read that book. Imagine being given one chance to guess right and then having to live with that choice for a week.

Furthermore, restricting a student to one book per visit will work against expanding student interests. Under such limitations, few students will risk wasting their one chance on an experiment. They'll be more likely to stick to the same kinds of books they've always read since they are *sure* they will like those.

Another practice that militates against recreational reading is that of allowing visits to the library only during the regularly scheduled class library period. Most readers don't automatically finish a book exactly one week after checking it out. Students in a recreational reading program shouldn't have to pace themselves through their reading matter. They should be able to gulp and gobble books, not just nibble as if they were on a 1000-word-a-day diet. Gluttony should be fostered in reading!

Librarians can give children the tools to easily find reading matter to their liking. Teachers and librarians should work together to provide instruction in using the card catalog; in learning about unusual reading matter, such as periodicals and pamphlets; and in knowing where different kinds of materials are shelved. As mentioned earlier, for some readers the slightest difficulty in locating material can spell the end of tentative efforts to try different kinds of reading.

Often children will ask the librarian to recommend a good book about tadpoles or a book that's funny. Unless the teacher has apprised the librarian of approximate reading levels of the students, the librarian may lead a child to an inappropriate book. Without specific information from teachers, librarians have only the children's grade placements to guide their recommendation. As a result, some children are needlessly embarrassed when they are directed to a book well beyond their reading ability.

If the school is small, librarians can quickly learn approximate reading levels for most students. In larger schools, however, teachers may share only the reading abilities of children well above or well below grade level.

In the same vein, librarians should be wary of considering certain books appropriate for particular age groups or kinds of children. A second grade friend of mine was once refused permission to check out a book because that book was for fourth and fifth graders. Self-selection should be the rule in the school library as well as in the classroom.

Librarians can also integrate the school library more fully into the recreational reading program by asking students to assist in ordering books for the library. Librarians can sponsor contests to identify the most popular books in specific categories. They can form student library councils, with rotating membership, for the purpose of eliciting student advice about what to order. Students can earn the privilege of ordering books by reading a certain number of books. The librarians can meet with children for Book Look Lunches and encourage them to talk about their preferences. In many ways, librarians can use their positions and their policies about the library to support the recreational reading program.

Motivational Activities for Librarians

In addition to setting policies that make recreational reading easy, librarians can be invaluable in efforts to motivate children to read. Because librarians work with all students in all grade levels, they may be the logical coordinators of schoolwide activities designed to encourage reading. For example, the library can house the scoreboard for reading contests involving several classrooms, keeping track of the number of books read in each classroom. (Hadden [1979] describes how kindergarten children and other nonreaders can participate fully in such schoolwide contests. These children are given credit for each book read *to* them at home. Hadden reports that these contests have spurred many parents to begin reading to their children in the evenings for the first time.) The librarian may be the neutral observer who gives the awards and impartially helps all contestants to find something to read.

Special displays within the library can be set up to stimulate the interest of the students in new topics or new genres. These displays should contain reading materials at a broad range of readability levels in order to meet the needs of all ages. After a week or so, the display could be "consumed." That is, children would be allowed to check out the books on display. Waiting lists for books might be compiled during the actual display period so that a mad rush on checkout day could be avoided. Furthermore, interested teachers could check the waiting lists themselves to gain information about the reading interests of their own students.

Some school librarians are willing to make up summer reading lists based on the public library's collections (Elsmo, 1978). In this way, the recreational reading program will not necessarily come to a halt when school is closed for the summer.

Better yet, in a few schools the library is opened one or two mornings a week during the summer, staffed by volunteer teachers, aides, and parents. The librarians in these schools could also volunteer for at least some of these sessions or could train volunteers to check out and reshelve materials according to the established system.

Librarians can also help involve students in reading on a schoolwide basis by giving the children worn or outdated reading materials that are being culled from the school's collection. Too often such materials are thoughtlessly incinerated. Many children would be delighted by the gift of a torn paperback with a page or two missing. It may be the only book they own.

Librarians can also become involved with individual classrooms. They can give Book Talks or tell stories. They can arrange for rotating monthly collections to augment classroom libraries. They can assist the teacher in developing a special collection of materials on a current social studies or science topic. They can just visit and reward recreational reading with a smile and "Oh, that's one of *my* favorite books, too."

Librarians are perhaps the most book-conscious individuals in a school. Most of them know well the majority of the materials in their care and can be wonderful resources for matching children and books. Teachers trying to develop recreational reading programs should try and tap these resources fully. They will find that most librarians will be simply delighted to extend their involvement.

Finding Materials for Children's Personal Libraries

Dishearteningly, many homes are completely devoid of reading materials. A large number of other homes may contain some adult reading matter—newspapers, magazines, *TV Guide*—but have nothing of interest to children. Teachers wanting to help their students develop the *habit* of reading should explore the many opportunities available for getting inexpensive books into home libraries.

RIF

One of the most exciting ways to get books into children's hands is the Reading Is Fundamental (RIF) program. RIF is a nationwide nonprofit organization, funded by the federal government, whose purpose is to motivate children to want to read by allowing them to select books to keep as their own.

Through the RIF program, local school systems and even private, nonprofit, and local agencies can apply for matching funds to purchase books for free distribution to children. At present, RIF will match funds at an incredible 3:1 ratio. In other words, for every dollar of local funds raised, RIF will contribute three dollars. (Federal funds, such as through Title I, may not be used as the local "seed money.")

Unlike many outside agencies, RIF appears to be relatively easy to deal with and straightforward. Thompson (1979) reports that RIF "imposes few constraints on local school systems, dispenses funds promptly, and absorbs the paperwork instead of passing it on to the schools" (p. 36). In fact, RIF emphasizes the use of volunteers, especially parents, in setting up and running the program. Although the primary purpose of utilizing volunteers is to increase community involvement in reading, the serendipitous outcome is that RIF does *not* demand a great deal from teachers.

Anyone wishing to initiate a RIF program must submit a proposal and must agree to several very sensible guidelines. For example, a minimum of three free book distributions must be held a year and *each* child must receive at least three books a year. The children are to be allowed to select their books without any adult interference. All RIF funds are to be used for purchasing books; administrative costs are to be the responsibility of the local sponsor. Because the primary purpose of the program is to show that reading is fun, RIF insists that "a continuous series of. . . book-related activities, before, during and after distributions, are a necessary part of the ongoing motivational process" (RIF manual, p. I-1).

In 1979, 2400 local RIF programs were funded, two-thirds of these sponsored by local public school systems (Thompson, 1979). RIF offers a complete manual for those desiring to apply for funds. The manual includes information on raising local funds, recruiting and utilizing volunteers, choosing and ordering books, and educating the public about reading. The manual may be obtained without cost from:

The Field Staff
Reading Is Fundamental, Inc.
Smithsonian Institution
475 L'Enfant Plaza #4800
Washington, D.C. 20560
Telephone: 202-381-6117

Other Ways to Augment Home Libraries
Several sources of inexpensive new and used books, such as book clubs and secondhand book shops, have already been described. These sources can be very useful in helping children to

start and increase their own personal libraries. Teachers can further aid the nurturance of home libraries in several other ways. For example, they can provide the students with opportunities to change the make-up of their libraries through trading. Petre (1971) reports that "book-swapping has become epidemic" (p. 192) in his secondary school. Teachers can foster swapping by setting up structured exchange sessions. One very simple way of organizing a book swap is described by Lowe (1977). All of the exchanging took place in one large room. As a child entered the room, the number of books he or she brought to the session was noted on a card. Then the child was allowed to take that many books out of the room. Simple.

Book swapping permits individuals to add new books to their libraries without having to spend any money. After the initial cost of getting some books (and in the case of RIF programs, there is no cost), the library is maintained primarily through swapping.

Teachers can add to their students' home libraries by giving away outdated texts that are scheduled for oblivion. They can also routinely cull old periodicals from the classroom library and allow the children to take these tattered treasures home. For a very modest cost, subscriptions to two or three children's magazines can be obtained. At the end of six months, the classroom library may have as many as 18 somewhat exhausted magazines and every month the teacher can give away the three oldest magazines through lottery or reward systems and still maintain the magazine inventory at 18.

If recreational reading is to extend outside of school, students must have access to something to read at home. Public libraries are an obvious source of reading material, but the reading habit will be instilled even more deeply if children begin to develop pride in ownership of books and in their home libraries.

KEEPING TRACK OF IT ALL

As you might suspect by now if you have read the rest of the book, this is going to be a very short section. Teachers who actually *like* making charts and checking things on lists and in general enjoy bookkeeping tasks can find lots to make them happy in a recreational reading program. They can keep track of how much each child has read; what was read; when it was read; to what degree it was comprehended by the reader; whether the student enjoyed it; and if the reader found the material too easy, too hard, or just right. They can develop systems that tell them which books are out of the classroom library, who has the books, and for how long. Undoubtedly, some of this recordkeeping may strengthen a recreational reading program by allowing the teacher to be aware of how much the children are actually reading and what they like to read. To those teachers who find enjoyment in keeping such records, I say, "Fine. Go to it. *But* be sure you are not interfering with self-selection and that you are not placing so much pressure on the *children* to keep records that they will learn to dislike reading."

To those teachers who find recordkeeping an odious burden, I offer this comfort: Probably the only kind of record you *must* keep is some sort of tally that will aid you in selecting books of interest to your current batch of children. If you suspect some of your students are not reading at all or that they consistently have poor comprehension, find a moment every week to chat with those students. You'll get your answer just as easily through these informal, spontaneous discussions as through more formal measures.

So I am ending this booklet with one final guideline. Keep in mind that recreational reading is supposed to be fun for everyone. If any aspect of recordkeeping interferes with or lessens the joy of reading, either for the students or for the teacher, then it should be dispensed with. Keep your recreational reading program simple, or it simply won't work.

References

Abrahamsen, R. Children's lit is a gold mine—help kids dig it. *Instructor*, 1977, *87*, 46.

Arlin, M., & Roth, G. Pupils' use of time while reading comics and books. *American Educational Research Journal*, 1978, *15*(2), 201-216.

Aronson, E., Blaney, N., Sikes, J., Stephan, C., & Snapp, M. The jigsaw route to learning and liking. *Psychology Today*, 1975, *8*, 43-50.

Bissett, D.J. The amount and effect of recreational reading in selected fifth grade classes. (Doctoral dissertation, Syracuse University, 1969.) *Dissertation Abstracts International*, 1969, 30, 5157-A. (University Microfilms No. 7010316)

Brown, D.H., Engin, A.W., & Wallbrown, F.H. Developmental changes in reading attitudes during the intermediate grades. *Journal of Experimental Education*, 1979, *47*, 259-262.

Brutton, D. How to develop and maintain student interest in reading. *English Journal*, 1974, *63*, 74-77.

Cain, M.A. Born to read: Making a reading culture. *Teacher*, 1978, *95*, 64-66.

California Reading Association. Idea bonanza: Reading. *Learning*, 1977, *6*, 45.

Coil, S.M. Paperbacks and progress against illiteracy. *School Library Journal*, 1978, *24*, 35-37.

Cox, C. Shakespeare and company: The best in classroom reading and drama. *Reading Teacher*, 1980, *33*(4), 438-441.

Criscuolo, N.P. Book reports: Twelve creative alternatives. *Reading Teacher*, 1977, *30*(8), 893-895.

Criscuolo, N.P. 25 ways to motivate the reluctant reader. *School and Community*, 1979, *65*, 13-16.

Eisenberg, M., & Notowitz, C. Book talks: Creating contagious enthusiasm. *Media & Methods*, 1979, *15*, 32-33.

Eller, W., & McClenathan, D. Corner on reading. *Early Years*, 1978, *8*, 19-20.

Elsmo, N. The library's role in reading for enjoyment. *Wisconsin State Reading Association Journal*, 1978, *22*(4), 20-24. (ED155656)

Faller, B.A., Jr. The basic basic: Getting kids to read. *Learning*, 1978, *6*, 100-101.

Flowers, C. Read for a balloon. *Instructor*, 1977, *87*, 44.

Gambrell, L.B. Getting started with sustained silent reading and keeping it going. *Reading Teacher*, 1978, *32*(3), 328-331.

Greaney, V., & Quinn, J. Factors related to amount and type of leisure time reading. Paper presented at the Seventh IRA World Congress on Reading, Hamburg, 1978. (ED163402)

Guthrie, J. Research views: Comics. *Reading Teacher*, 1978, *32*(3), 377-378.

Hadden, M.S. Mid-year blahs? Try a reading contest. *School Library Journal*, 1979, *25*, 42.

Hamilton, H. TV tie-ins as a bridge to books. *Language Arts*, 1976, *53*(2), 129-130.

Heathington, B.S. What to do about reading motivation in the middle school. *Journal of Reading*, 1979, *22*(8), 709-713.

Higgins, J., & Kellman, A. I like Judy Blume. It's like she knows me. *Teacher*, 1979, *96*, 72-74.

Hunt, L.C., Jr. The effect of self-selection, interest, and motivation upon independent, instructional, and frustrational levels. *Reading Teacher*, 1970, *24*(2), 146-151, 158.

Hunter, J. Hooks to catch "on level" readers. *Reading Teacher*, 1980, *33*(4), 467-468.

Indrisano, R. Reading: What about those who can read but don't? *Instructor*, 1978, *87*, 94-98.

Kean, M.H., Summers, A.A., Raivetz, M.J., & Farber, I.J. *What works in reading?* Philadelphia: Office of Research and Evaluation, School District of Philadelphia, 1979.

Kraus, H.F., & Haas, E. Reading is a three-ring circus. *Instructor*, 1977, *87*, 43.

Lamme, L. Are reading habits and abilities related? *Reading Teacher*, 1976, *30*(1), 21-27.

Ley, T.C. Getting kids into books: The importance of individualized reading. *Media & Methods*, 1979, *15*, 22-24.

Long, B.H., & Henderson, E.H. Children's use of time: Some personal and social correlates. *Elementary School Journal*, 1973, *73*, 193-199.

Lough, P. Going... going... gone for reading! *Teacher*, 1979, *96*, 60-61.

Lowe, B.R. Book swap shop. *Instructor*, 1977, *87*, 47.

Lowery, L.F., & Grafft, W. Paperbacks and reading attitudes. *Reading Teacher*, 1968, *21*(7), 618-623.

McCracken, R.A. Initiating sustained silent reading. *Journal of Reading*, 1971, *41*(8), 521-524, 582-583.

McCracken, R.A., & McCracken, M.J. Modeling is the key to sustained silent reading. *Reading Teacher*, 1978, *31*(4), 406-408.

McEachern, W.R. Reading attitudes of adult Native Indian students. *Journal of Reading*, 1980, *23*(5), 390.

Negin, G.A. Comic books in perspective. *Wisconsin State Reading Association Journal*, 1978, *22*(4), 5-11. (ED155656)

Pelletier, C. World of books: Story settings take kids touring. *Learning*, 1979, *7*, 77.

Petre, R.M. Reading breaks made it in Maryland. *Journal of Reading*, 1971, *15*(3), 191-194.

Rathbun, D. How to get middle schoolers to read when they're not thrilled about the idea and you're not too thrilled about the idea and you're not too sure about what to do anyway. *Learning*, 1977, *6*, 122-136.

Practice

Reading Is Fundamental, Inc. *Resource manual for inexpensive book distribution programs for reading motivation.* Washington, D.C.: Office of Education, Department of Health, Education and Welfare, 1979.

Roeder, H.H., & Lee, N. Twenty-five teacher-tested ways to encourage voluntary reading. *Reading Teacher*, 1973, *27*(1), 48-50.

Roettger, D. Elementary students' attitudes toward reading. *Reading Teacher*, 1980, *33*(4), 451-454.

Rosler, F. Spring reading campaign at P.S. 183. *Reading Teacher*, 1979, *32*(4), 397-398.

Ross, P.A. Getting books into those empty hands. *Reading Teacher*, 1978, *31*(4), 397-399.

Ryan, J. Family patterns of reading problems: The family that reads together.... *Claremont College Reading Conference Yearbook*, 1977, *41*, 159-163.

Sauls, C.W. The relationship of selected factors to the recreational reading of sixth grade students. (Doctoral dissertation, Louisiana State University and Agricultural and Mechanical College, 1971.) *Dissertation Abstracts International*, 1971, 32, 2558-A. (University Microfilms No. 7129390)

Smith, R., & Johnson, D. *Teaching Children to Read.* Reading, Mass.: Addison-Wesley, 1976.

Stanchfield, J.M., & Fraim, S.R. A follow-up study on the reading interests of boys. *Journal of Reading*, 1979, *22*(8), 748-752.

Stevens, K.C. Trivia contest stimulates enthusiastic reading. *Reading Teacher*, 1980, *33*(4), 466-467.

Thompson, M. Reading is fundamental: A federal book program that saves money and works—without paperwork. *American School Board Journal*, 1979, *166*, 36-38.

Usova, G.M. Techniques for motivating interest in reading for the disadvantaged high school student. *Reading Improvement*, 1978, *15*, 36-38.

Watson, J.J. Picture books for young adolescents. *The Clearing House*, 1978, *51*, 208-212.

Wells, R. Parents and reading: What fifth graders report. *Journal of Research and Development in Education*, 1978, *11*(3), 20-26.

Williams, M. Mystery book bag. *Learning*, 1977, *6*, 59-60.

Yatvin, J. Recreational reading for the whole school. *Reading Teacher*, 1977, *31*(2), 185-188.